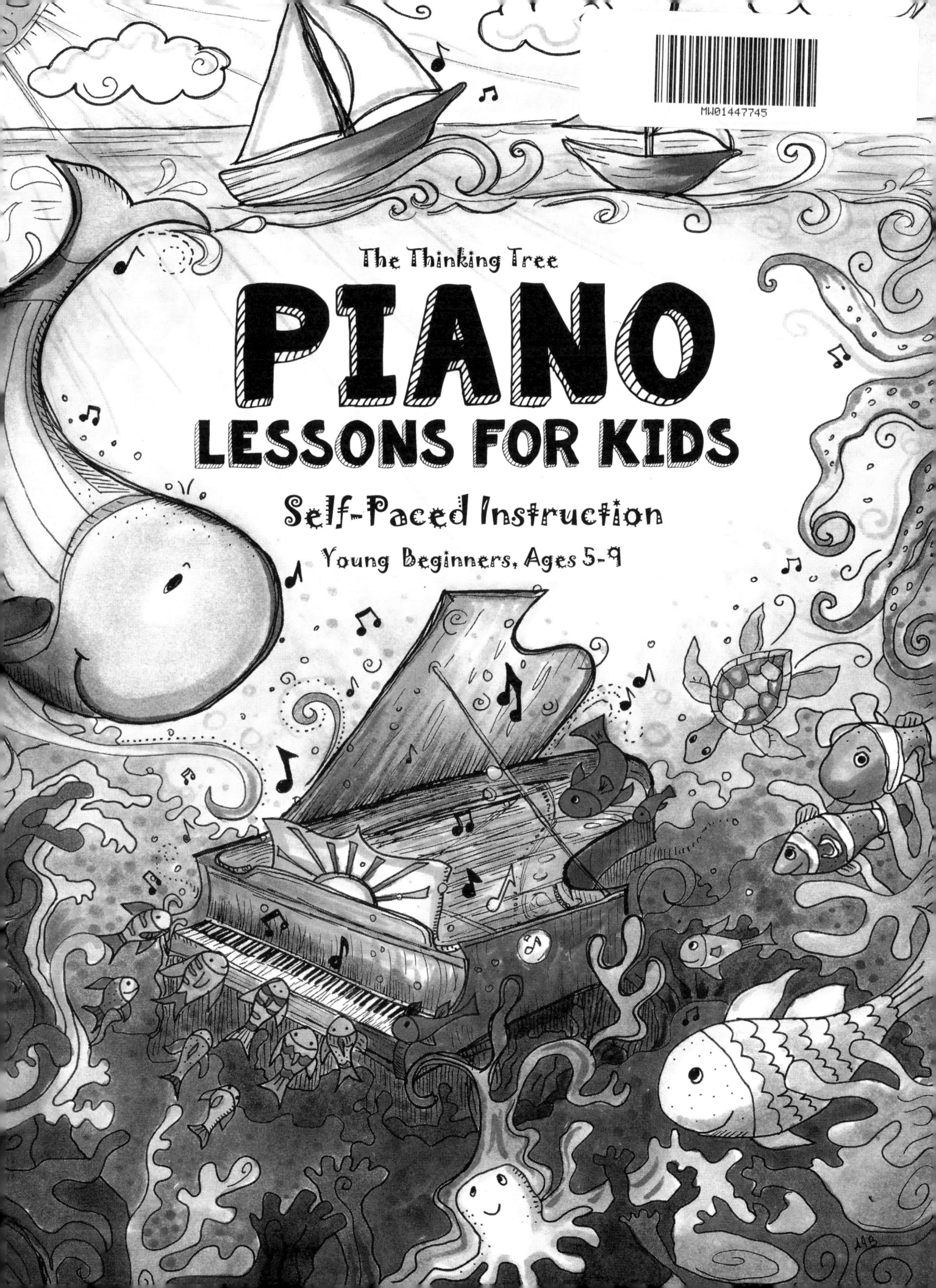

The Thinking Tree

PIANO
LESSONS FOR KIDS

Self-Paced Instruction

Young Beginners, Ages 5-9

THE THINKING TREE

The Thinking Tree
PIANO
LESSONS FOR KIDS

AUTHOR: AMBER ROBINSON

Illustrators: Sarah Janisse Brown, Alexandra Bretush, Anna Kidalova

Aquarium Illustration: Tolik Trishkin

Editing: Aaron J. Robinson

Copyright ©2018 Amber Robinson &

The Thinking Tree, LLC - All Rights Reserved

MY SONGS

Carnival of the Animals
by Camille Saint-Saëns

Page

Aquarium 24
Cuckoo 26
Fossils 28
The Swan 30
March of Royal Lions...................................48
Elephant 50

Performance Songs

Mary Had a Little Lamb................................78
Twinkle, Twinkle, Little Star........................ 118
Ode to Joy 120
Star Light, Star Bright 122
Westminster Chimes 126
Old MacDonald...128
Minuet in G 156

MY SONGS

Everyday Songs   Page
Bell Chimes 90
Sharks 94
Picnic 100
Swings 104
Aliens 108
Ocean Waves..114

Holiday Songs
Jingle Bells..124
Jolly Old St. Nicholas 132
Away in a Manger.....................................150
Joy to the World..152
Happy Birthday to You 154

Composed Songs
High-Middle-Low 74
Super Hero 134
Super Villain..148
Songs by Me..................................... 158–165

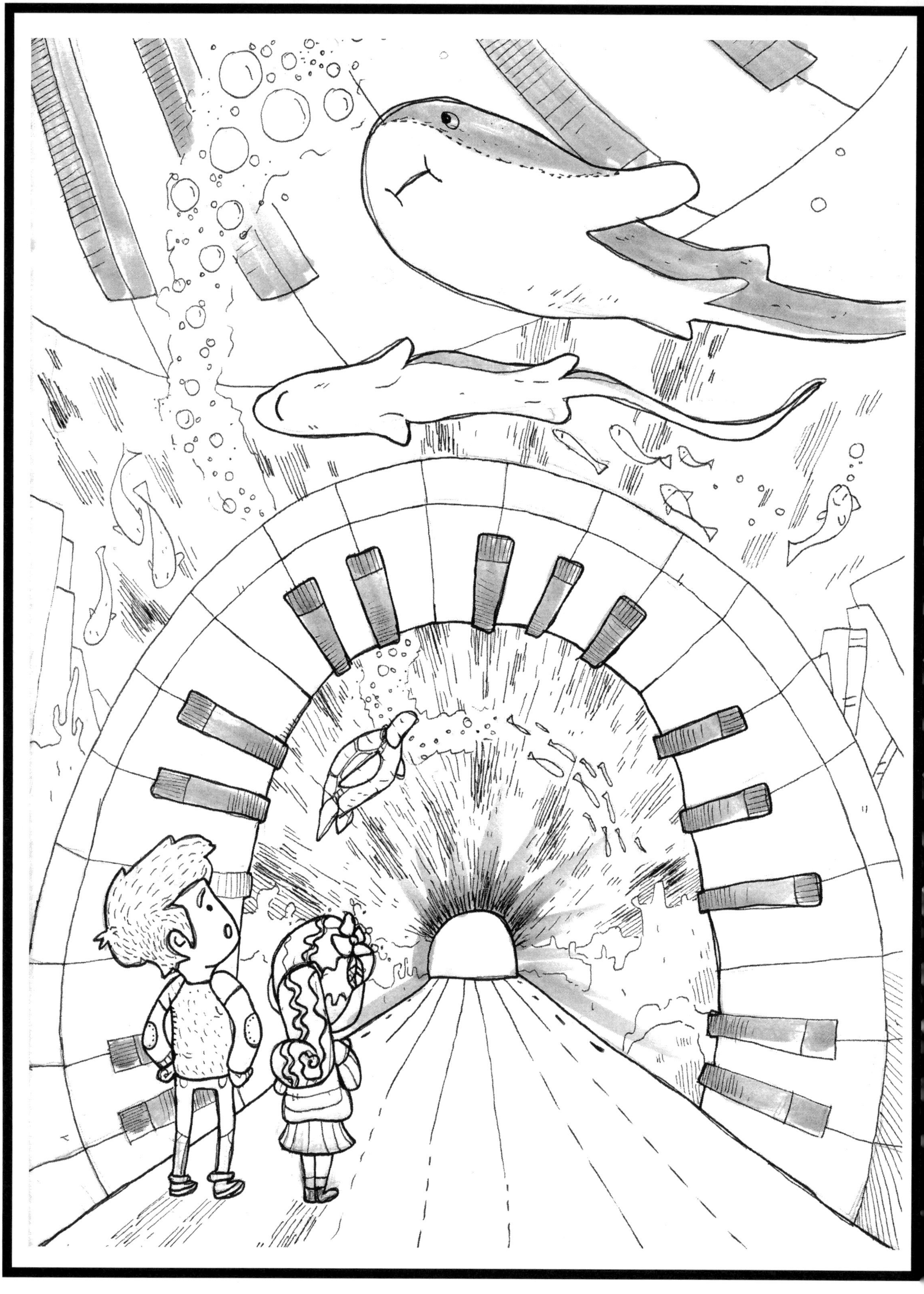

MUSIC IS WHAT WE HEAR!

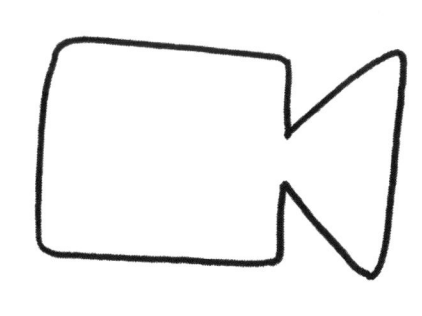

AUDIO TRACKS & VIDEO INSTRUCTION TO ACCOMPANY THIS BOOK:

amberrobinson.com/pianokids

The Thinking Tree, LLC

FunSchoolingBooks.com

Copyright 2018 – Do Not Copy

TEACHER'S NOTE:

I was once a little girl, captivated by the church's Baldwin grand piano in a small Indiana farming town. I vividly remember seeing the piano up close and "knowing" that I had to learn to play. My father, a local math teacher, "bought" me my first piano lesson at age 5 for a trade. He tutored the piano teacher's daughter in algebra during my lessons.

Many piano teachers came to town and moved away. And I cobbled together enough notes, rhythm, and technique, to find a spot in a university music school.

In college, a whole new world of pedagogy and sequence opened up to me. I remember wishing so badly I had learned this way as a child—with **PLAY/GAMES** and **CREATIVITY**. But most importantly, a clearly **SEQUENCED MAP**—from start to finish.

In college and post college training, I would learn **CLEAR SEQUENCING** and **SOLID TECHNIQUE** from the ideas of Dalcroze, Kodaly, Orff, Takadimi, Suzuki, Gordon, Faber, Paul Wirth's Gravity Technique, and Irina Gorin's Russian/Ukranian finger numbering.

This way of playing piano includes:

- Active **LISTENING** and **MOVEMENT** come first.
- **NOTE READING** comes **LAST** (just like in learning to speak your native language).
- **FINGER #**'s are different. (Start with "3's" for good technique.)
- We **HEAR, SING,** and **PLAY NOTES** before we learn piano **KEY LETTERS** or **STAFF** notes.
- We **SEE** music symbols long before they get **LABELS**.
- **CREATE** through **COMPOSING** and **IMPROVISING** right from the start.

Thank you for giving your child the gift of music! I am so grateful for you.
In 20 years of teaching, it never grows old to see students' joy as they learn piano and unleash their imaginations. Your exciting adventure starts now!

MUSIC LEARNING

Hear

Move

Speak

Sing

Tap

Play

Read

Write

(Improvise and Compose throughout)

Sounds
Sweep & Swoop

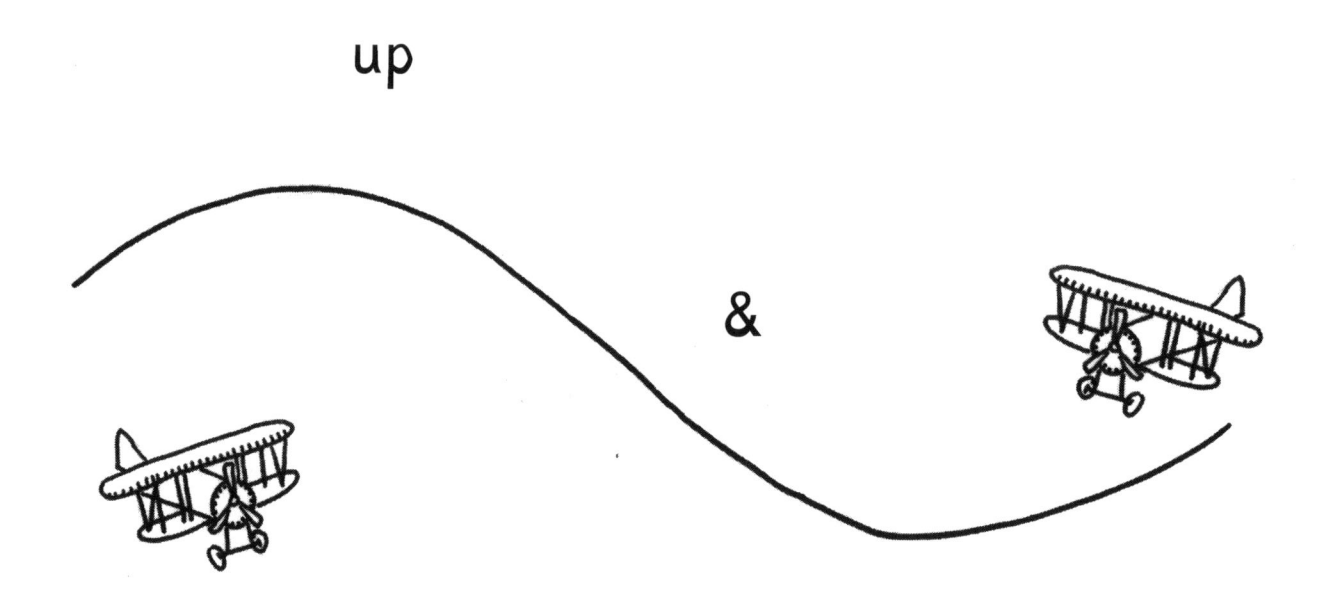

up

&

down

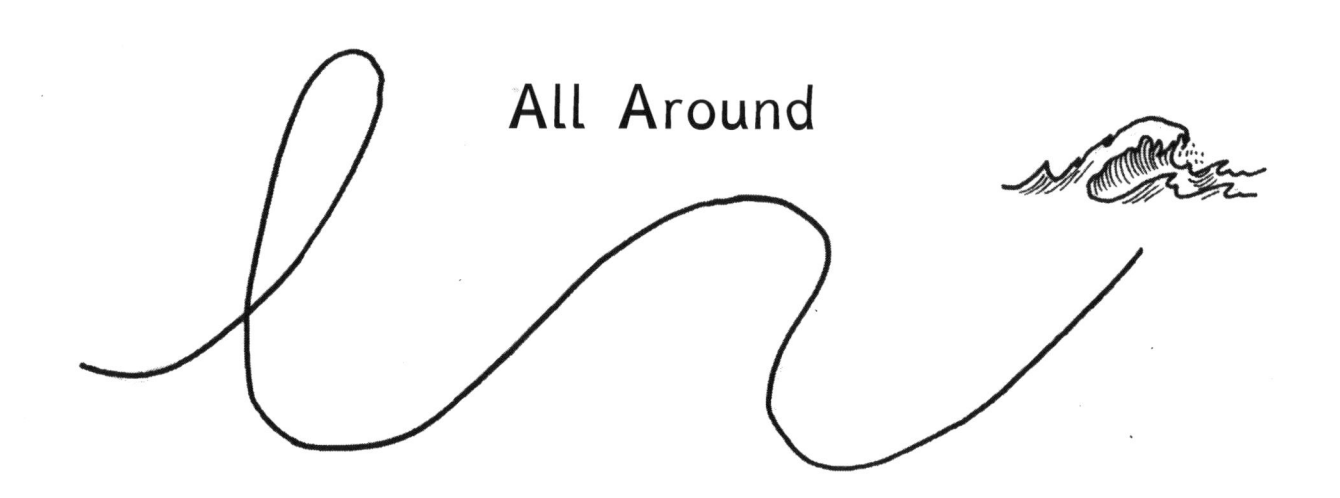

All Around

Bright

&

Happy

Bumpy

&

Grumpy

Jagged

&

Jumpy

I SEE A SOUND

Sounds that Stare...

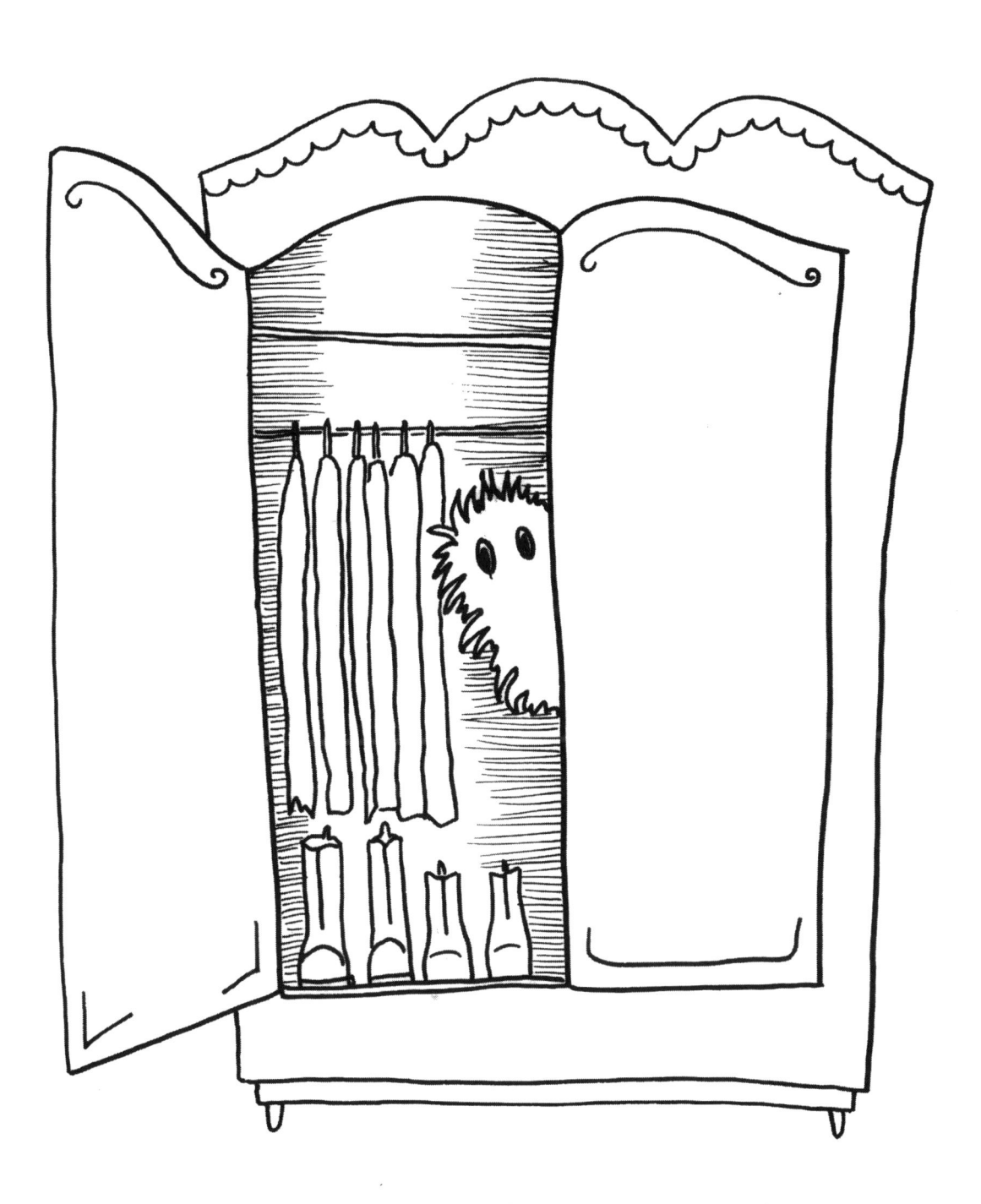

or barely there

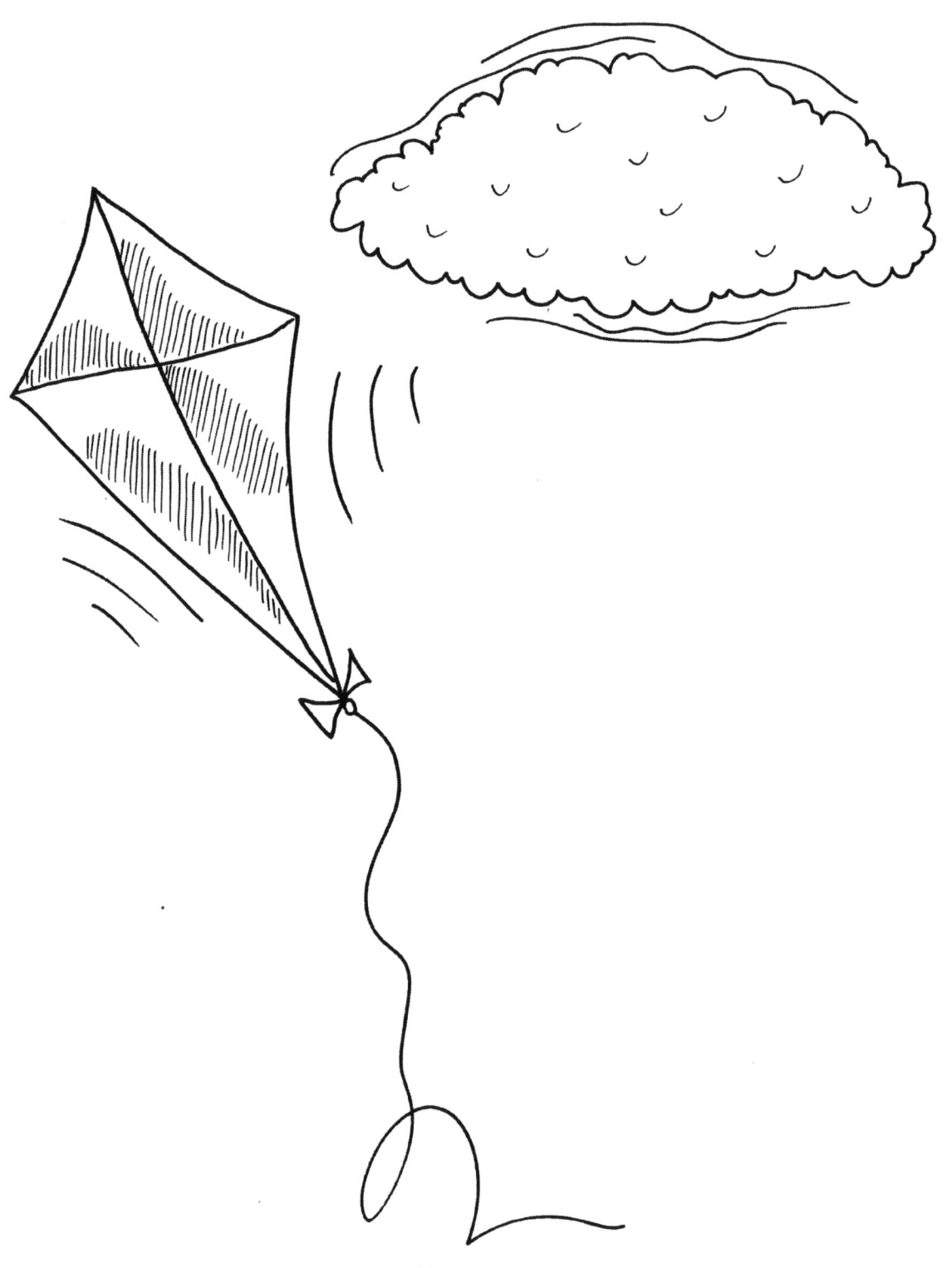

WHAT DOES A SOUND FEEL LIKE?

Trace each sound with your finger.

Pinchy

∧∧∧∧∧∧∧∧∧∧∧∧

or

Squishy

_____

Flat

or

Puffy

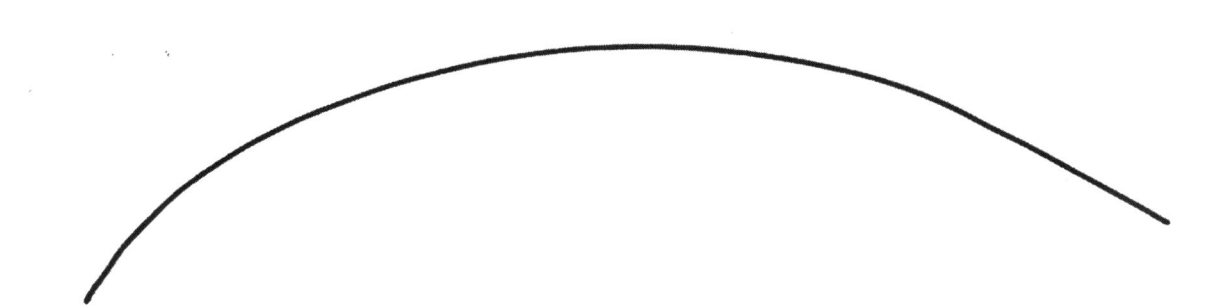

Smooth

or

Scratchy

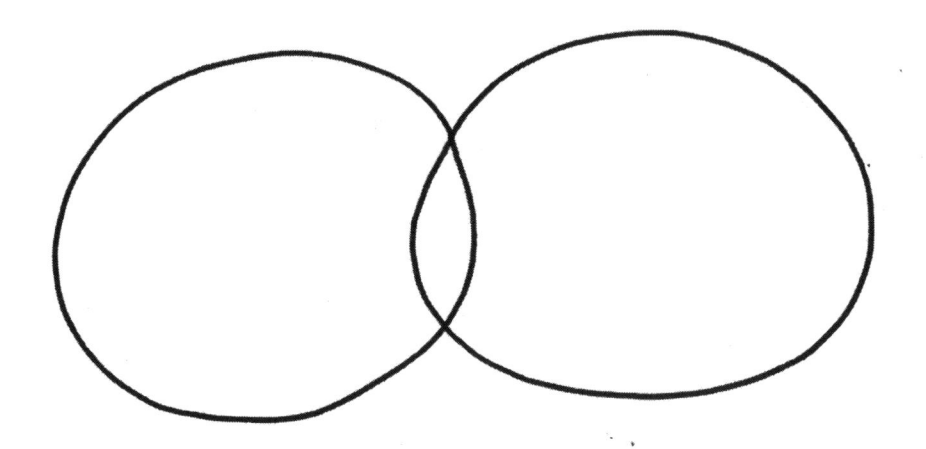

Huggy

or

Buggy

20

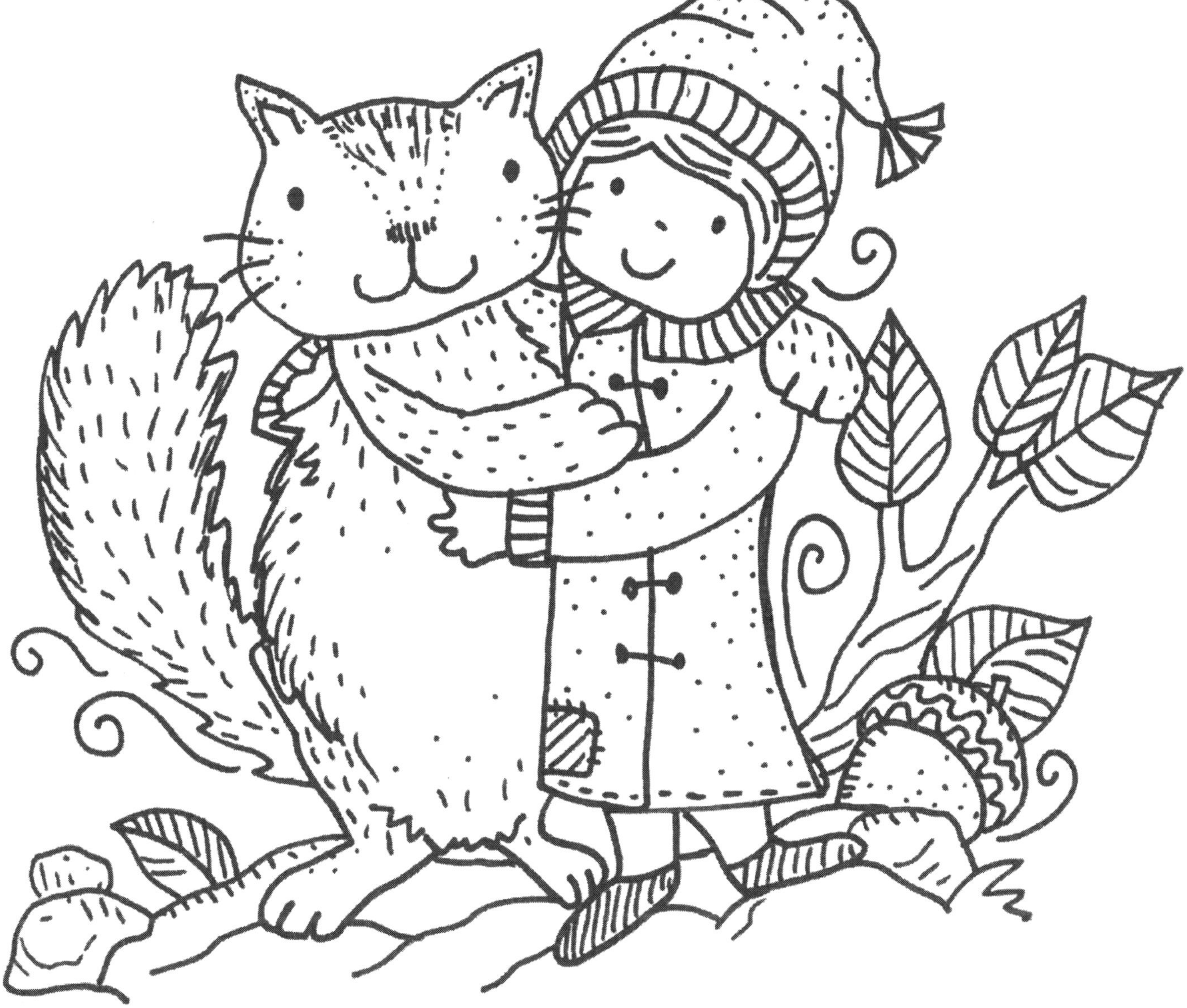

WHAT DOES A SOUND SMELL LIKE?

Imagine the smells that go with these sounds

SMOKY

WOODSY

SWEET

WHAT DOES A SOUND TASTE LIKE?

Draw your own

SOUR

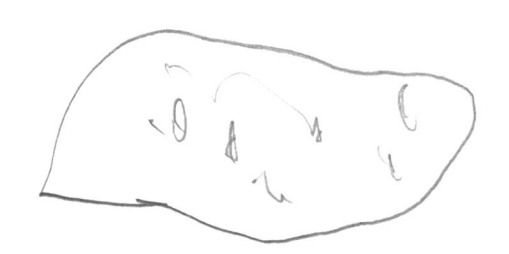

SALTY

SPICY

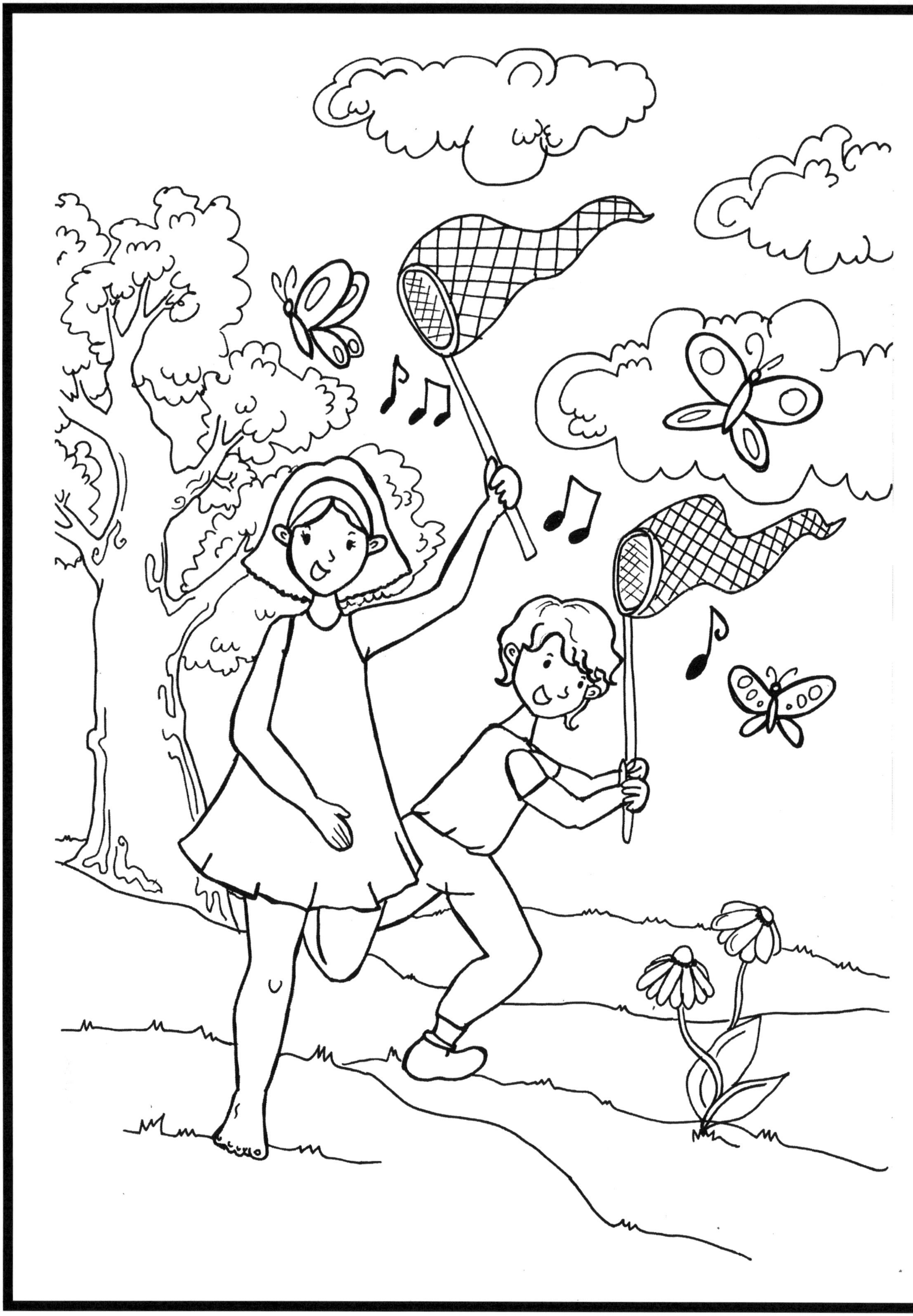

Find a colorful

Scarf

or

Ribbon

or

Flag

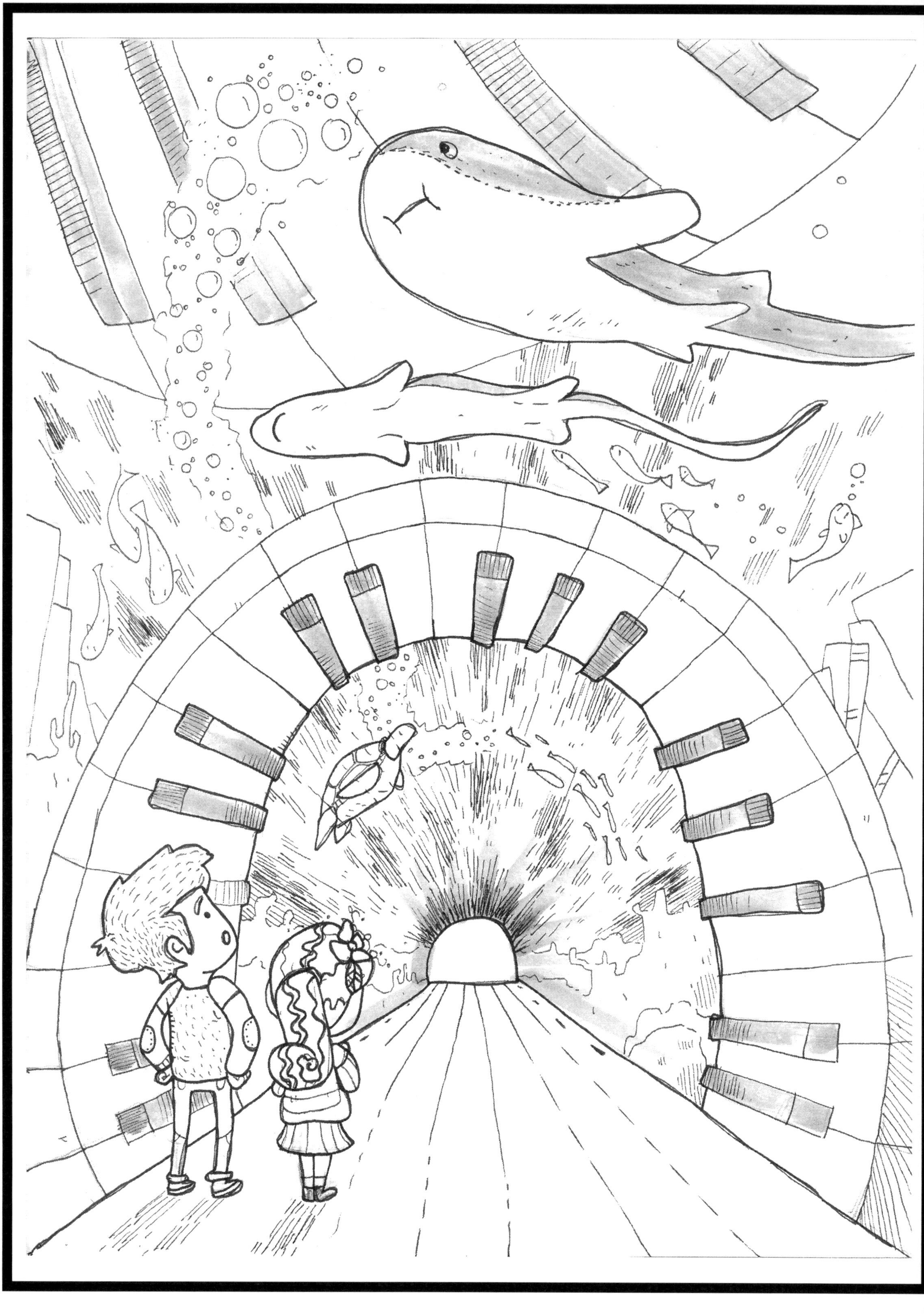

MOVE TO THE SOUNDS

HOLD
your scarf

&

MOVE
to the music.

AQUARIUM

Carnival of the Animals
by **Camille Saint-Saëns**

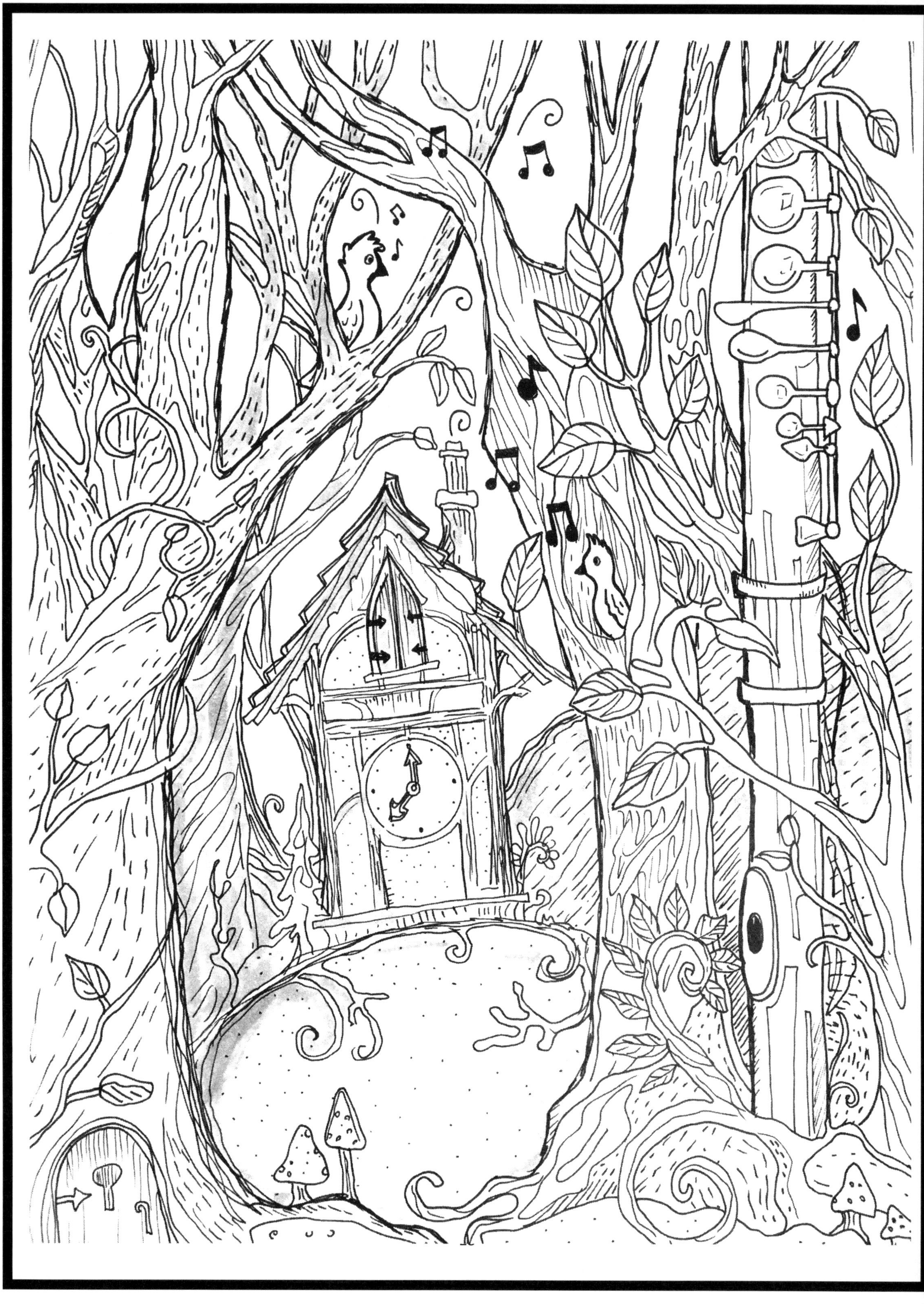

FLY like a

CUCKOO

bird

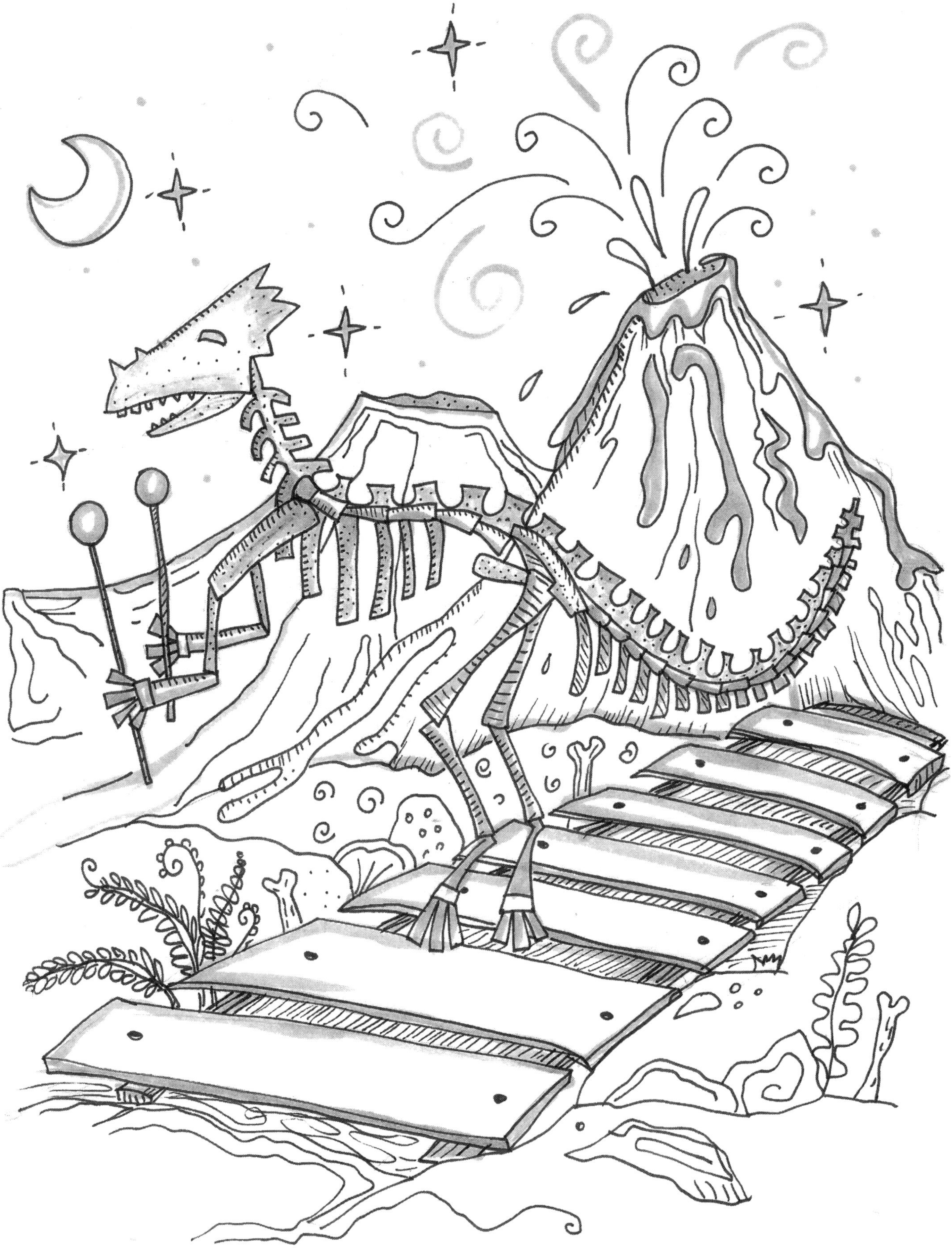

MOVE like the Dinosaur FOSSILS

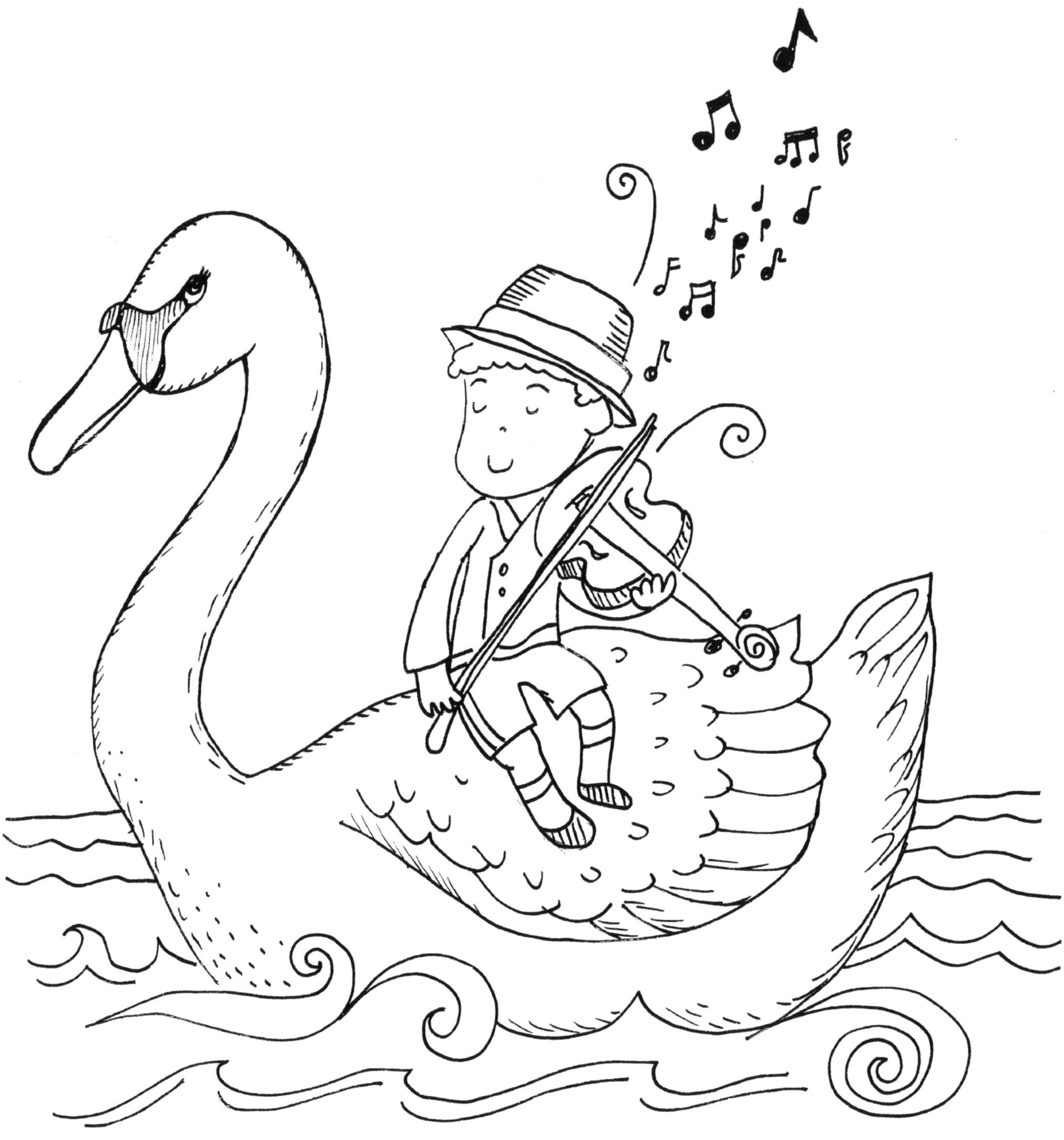

SWIM with THE SWAN

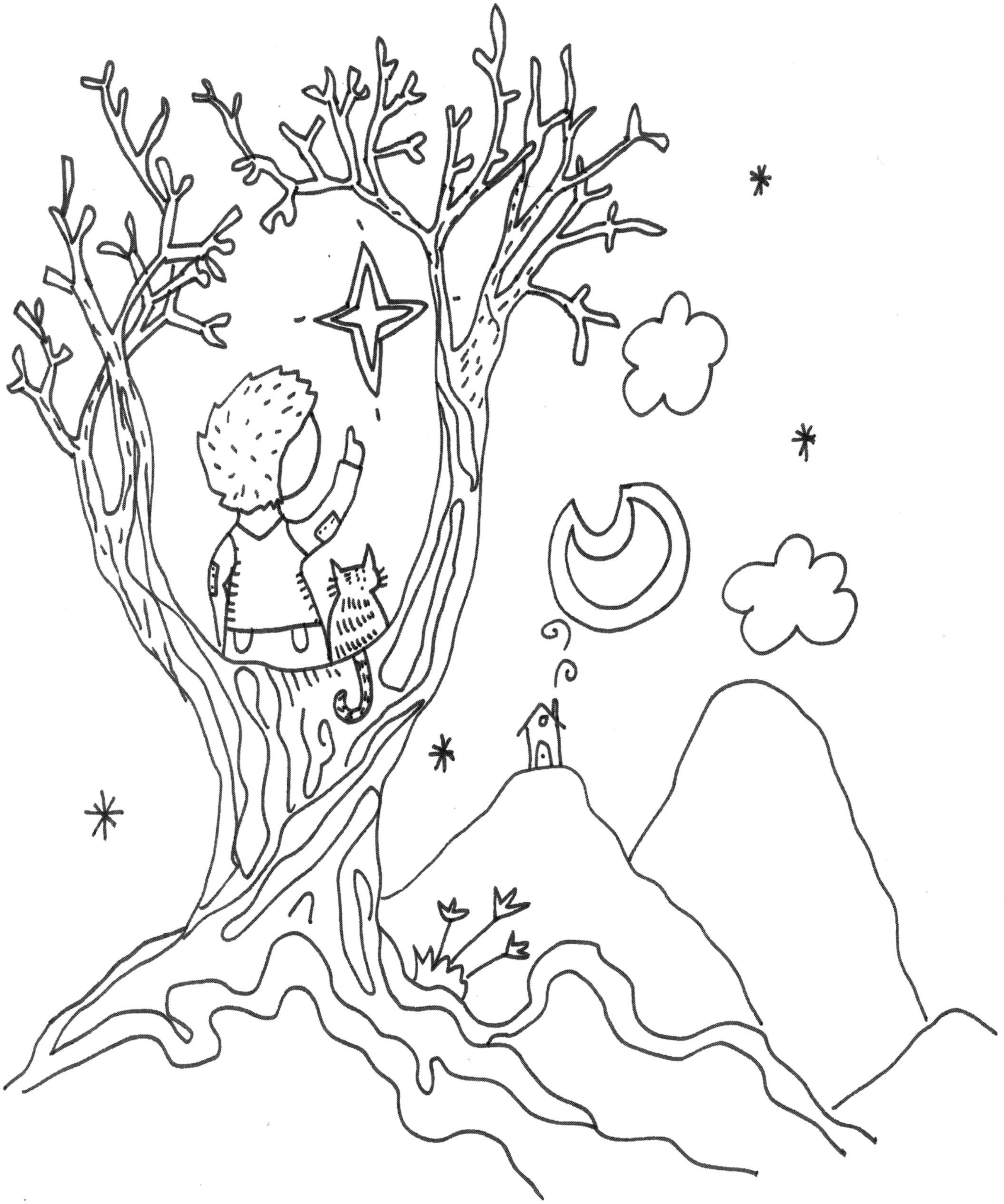

SPEAK THE SOUNDS

STAR LIGHT, STAR BRIGHT

Star light, star bright,

The first star I see tonight;

I wish I may, I wish I might,

Have the wish I wish tonight.

—Anonymous

SIT AT THE PIANO

Gravity makes fruit fall from a tree...

raise your arms...

Gravity makes them fall on the keys.

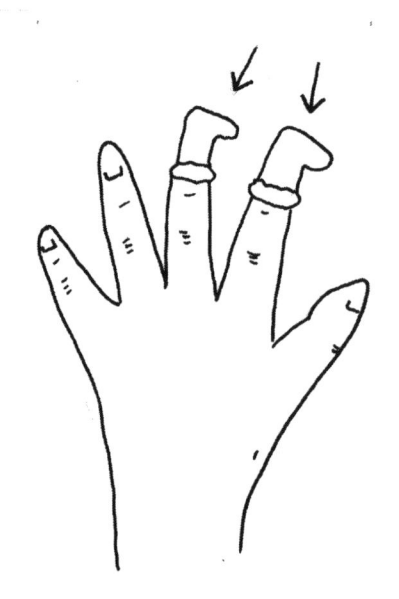

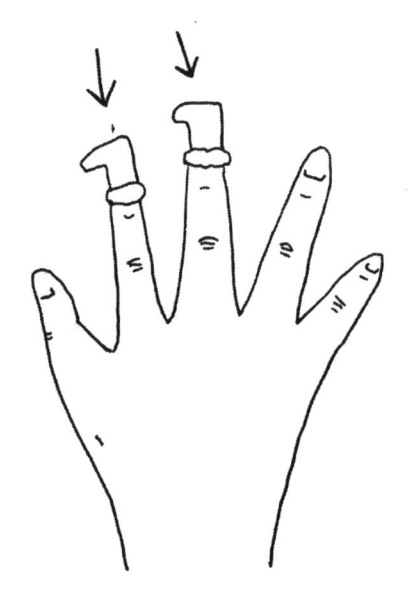

Imagine your "V" fingers
are the legs of a little person.

They JUMP together on the keys.

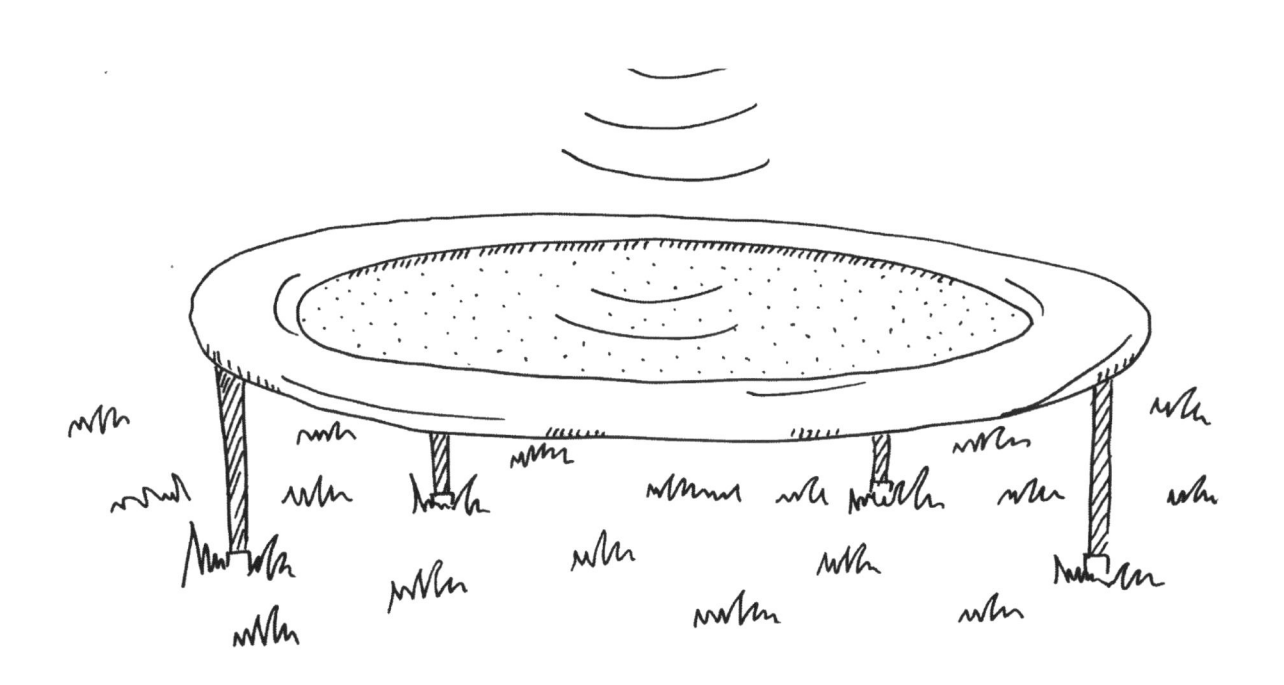

The bottom of the key bed is
their trampoline

Keep flexible wrists and arms.
And strong fingers.

WHAT MAKES A PIANO SOUND?

Open the lid...

and get a SURPRISE...

HAMMERS!

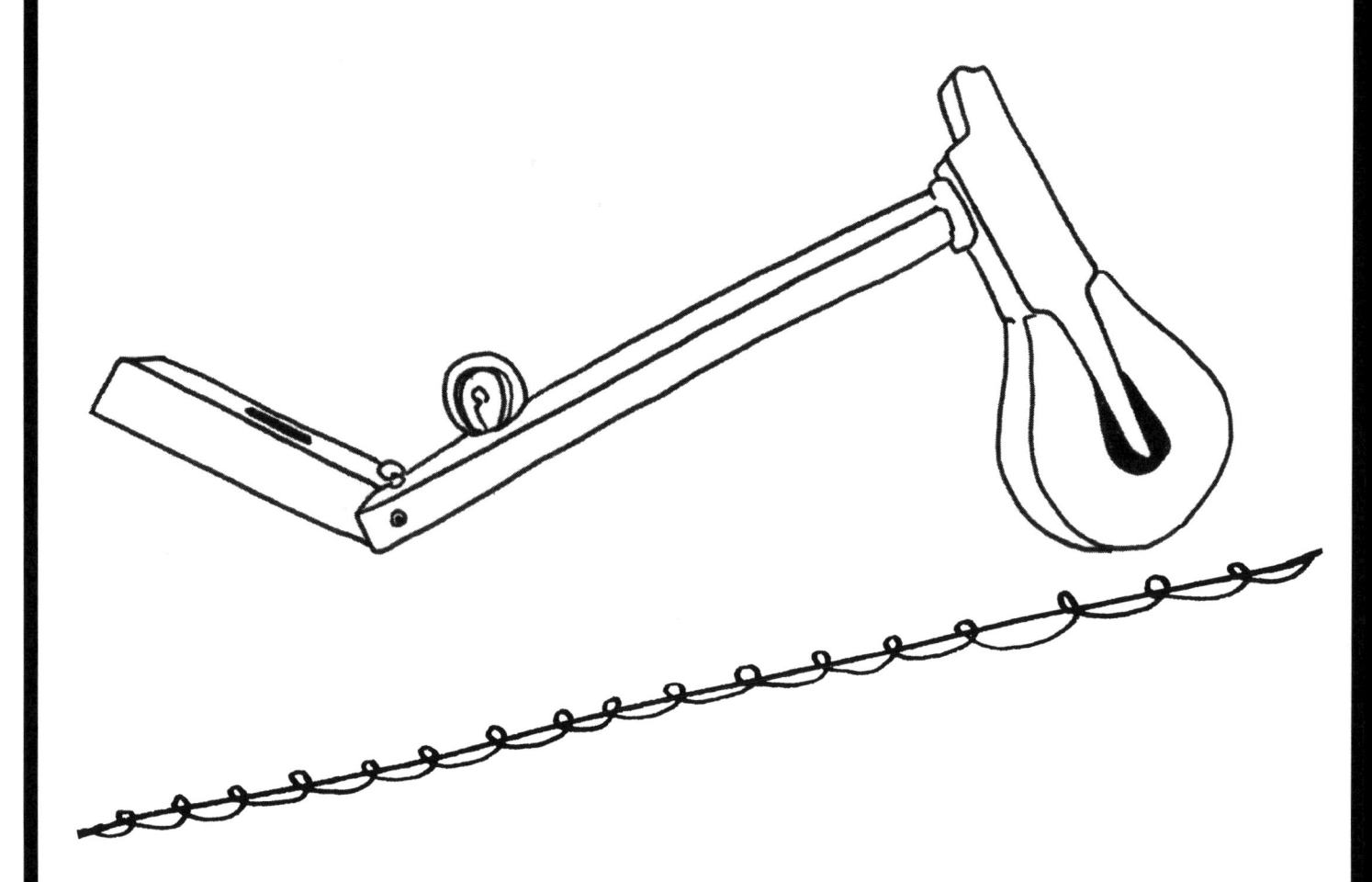

Hammers

wrapped in felt

hit strings

to make a sound

that travels to your ear.

HAMMER Sound =

♩ ♩ ♩ ♩

STEADY BEAT

Can you TAP

your HEART BEAT?

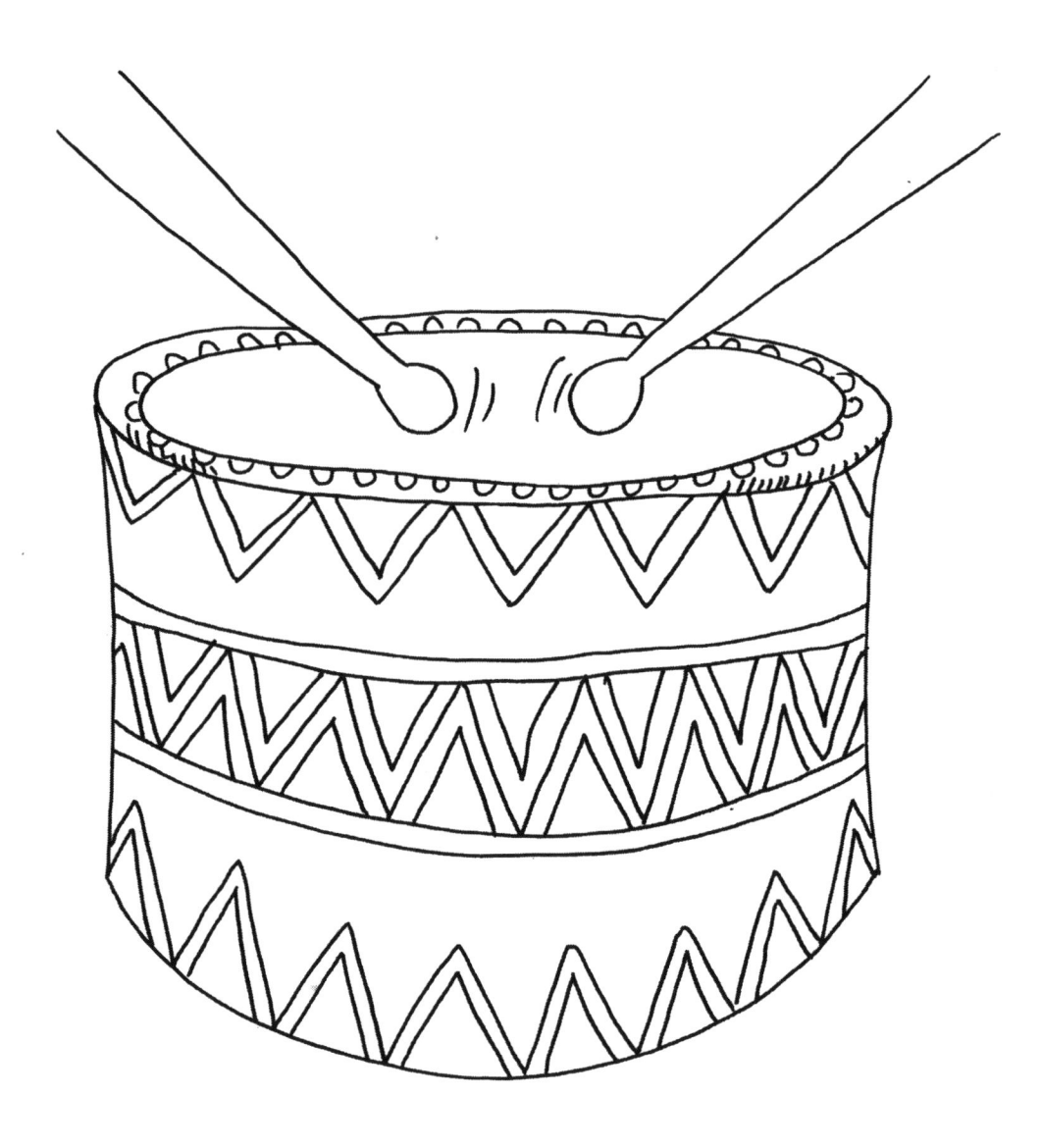

Can you DRUM

Can you CONDUCT

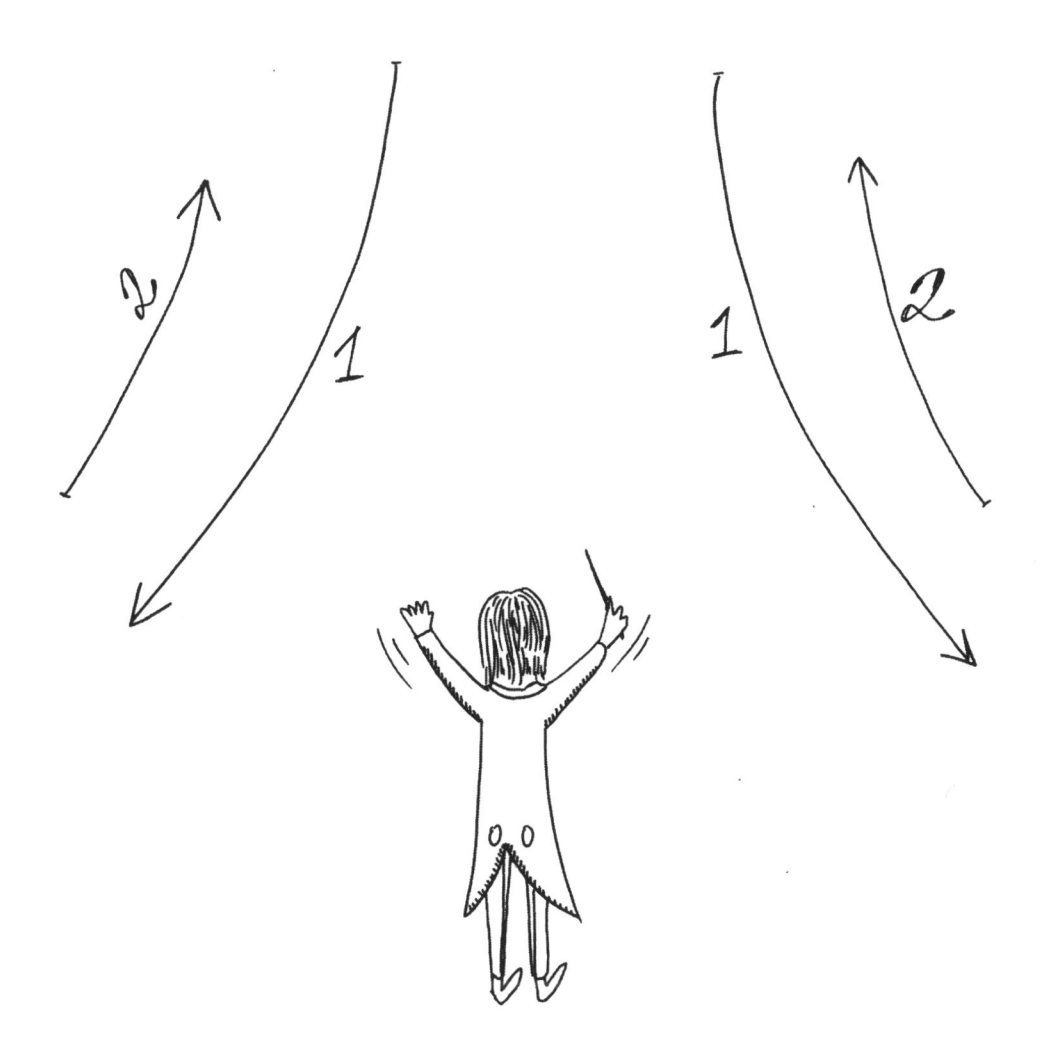

an orchestra

with a

STEADY BEAT?

50

MARCH your feet
to the STEADY BEAT.

MARCH OF THE ROYAL LIONS

Carnival of the Animals
by Camille Saint-Saëns

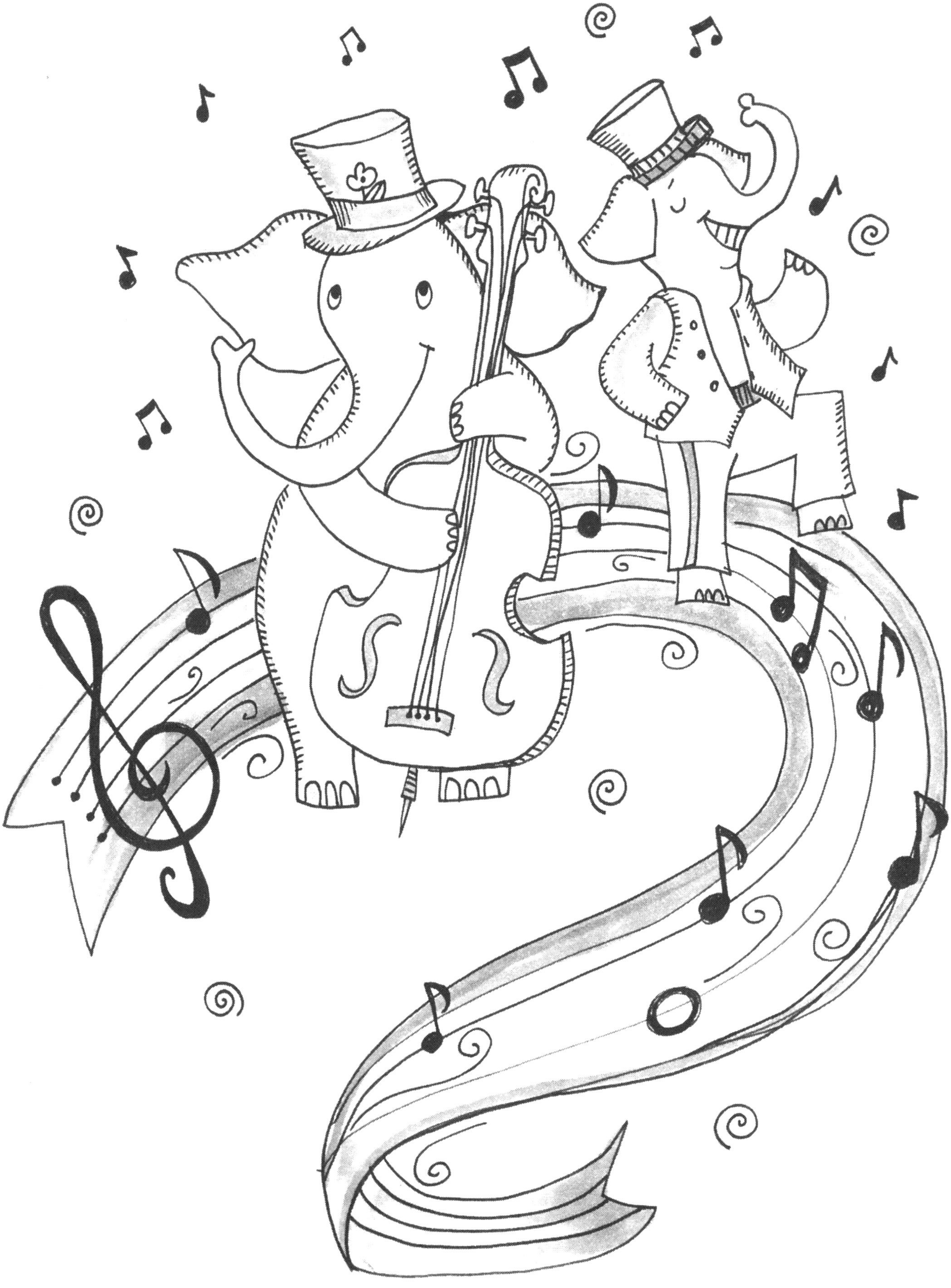

Stomp like an ELEPHANT
to the steady beat.

THE ELEPHANT

Carnival of the Animals
by Camille Saint-Saëns

PLAY a STEADY BEAT

With your "V" fingers on **TWO BLACK KEYS.**

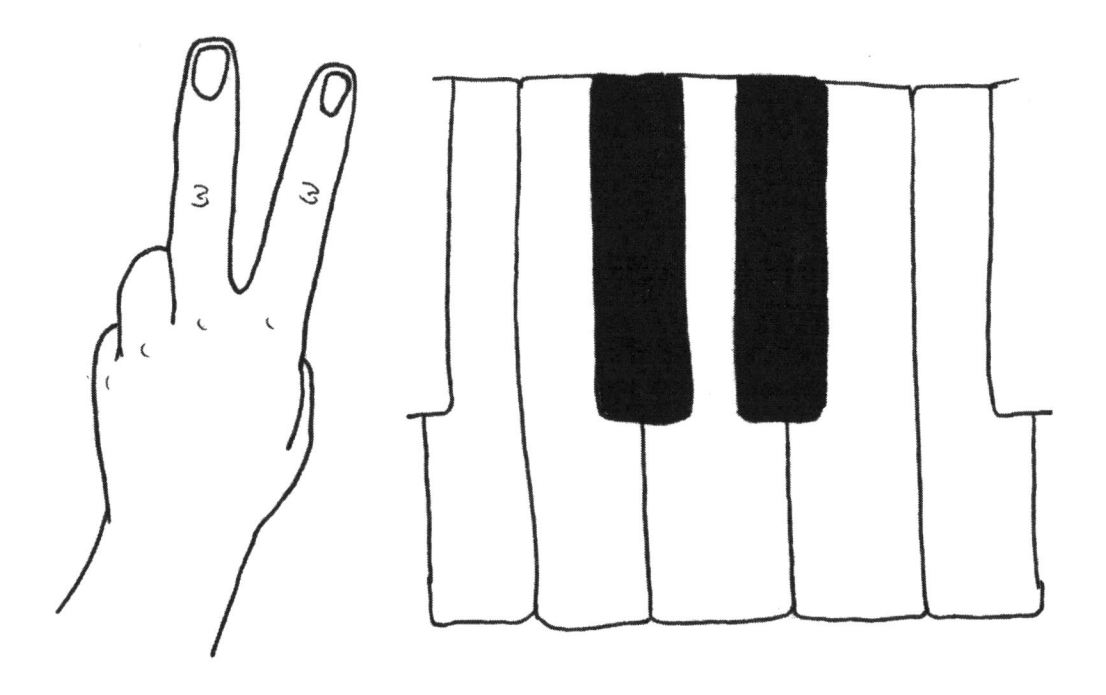

Play for your cat

or your sister

or your favorite stuffed animal

SING HIGH AND LOW SOUNDS

Whoooooo

Booooooo

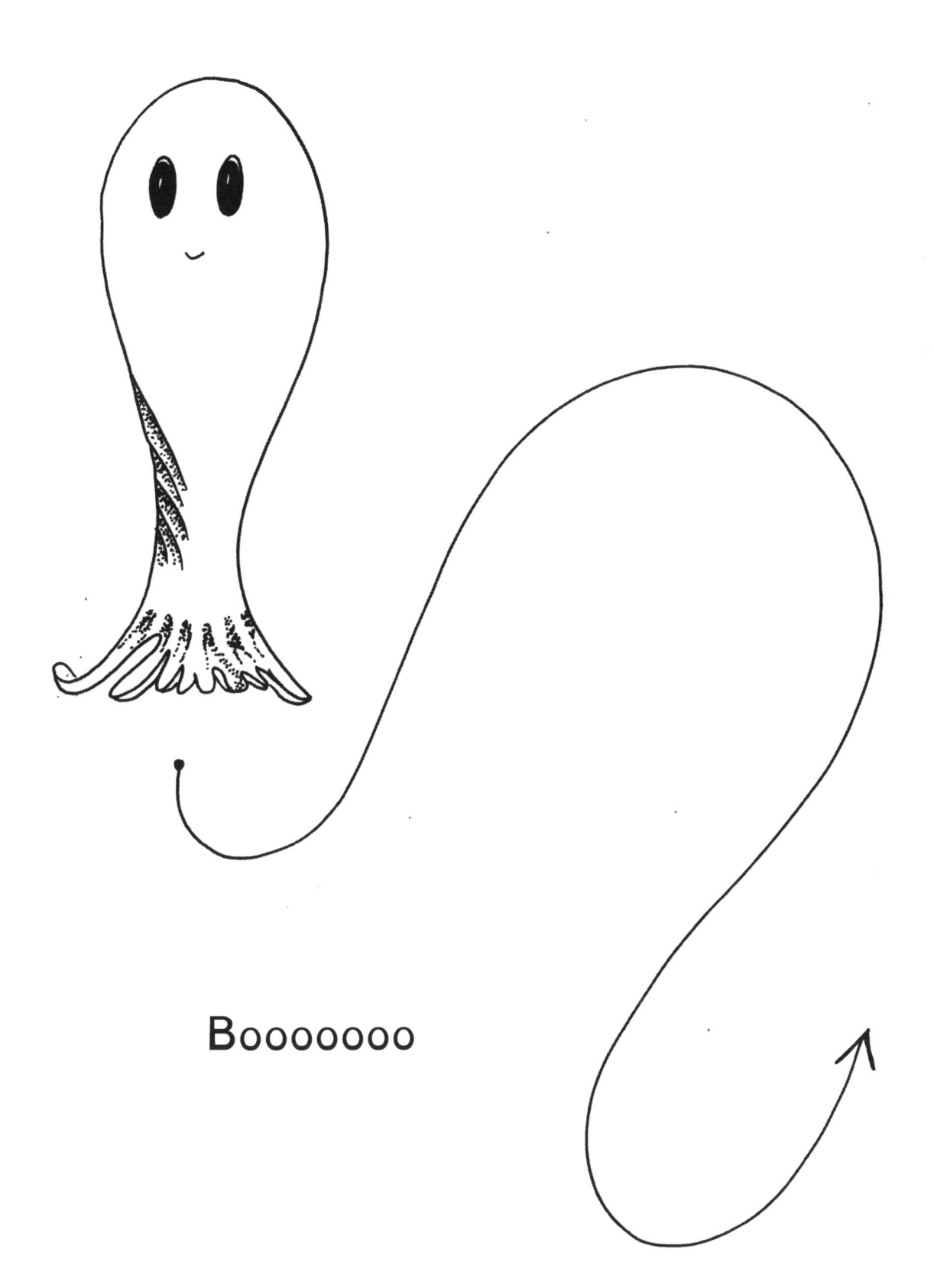

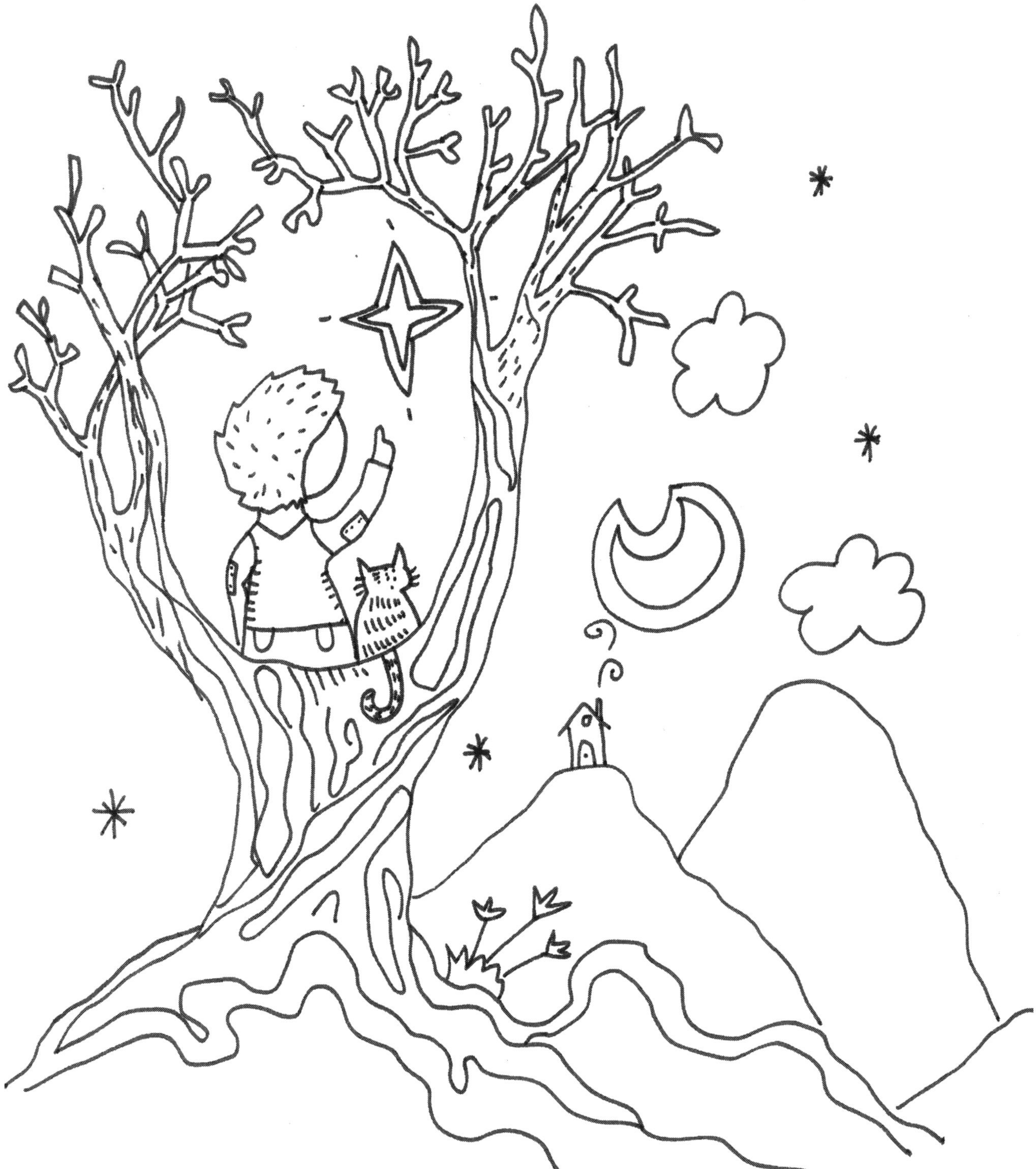

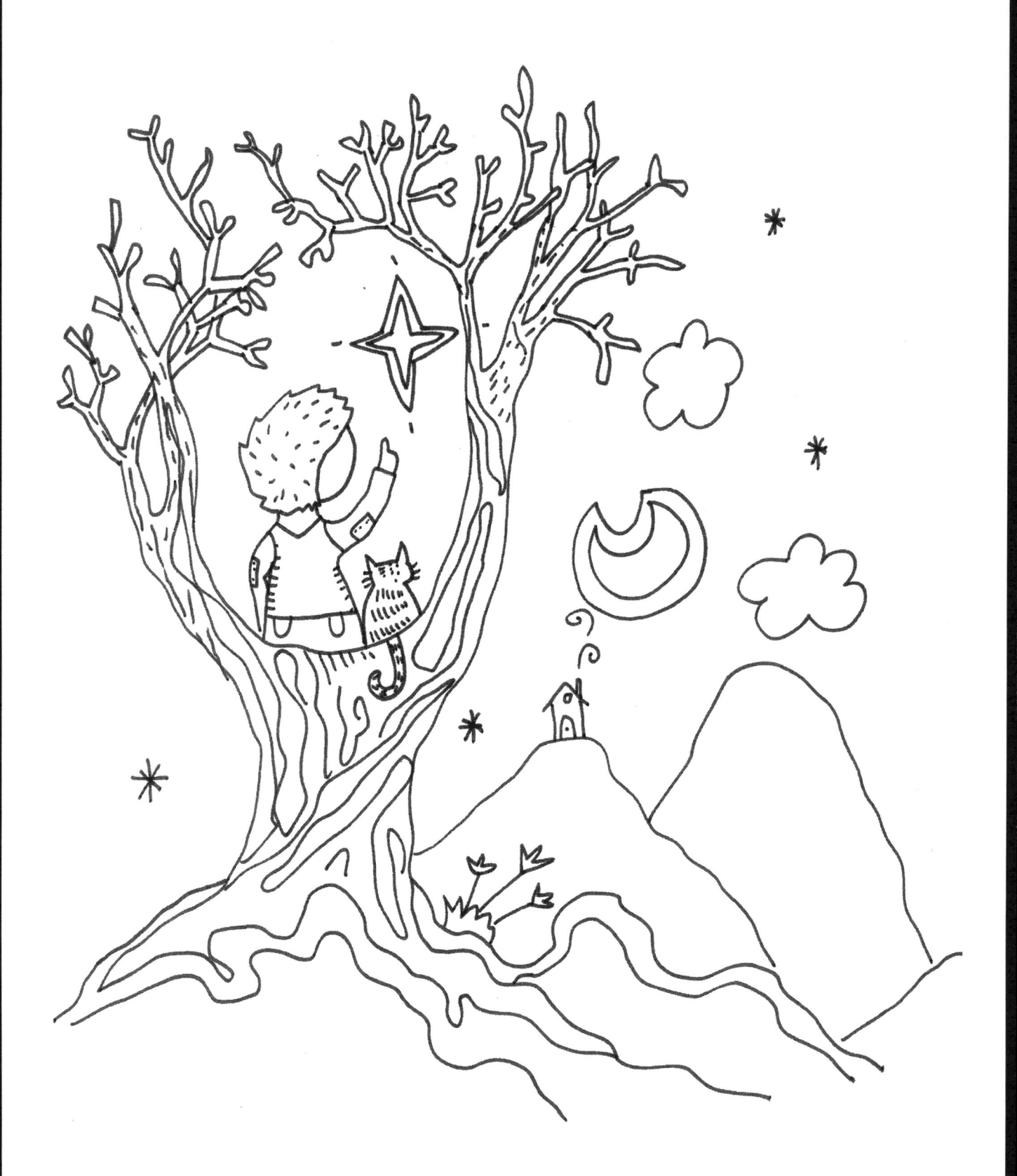

SING THE SOUNDS

STAR LIGHT, STAR BRIGHT

Star light, star bright,

The first star I see tonight;

I wish I may, I wish I might,

Have the wish I wish tonight.

                         - Anonymous

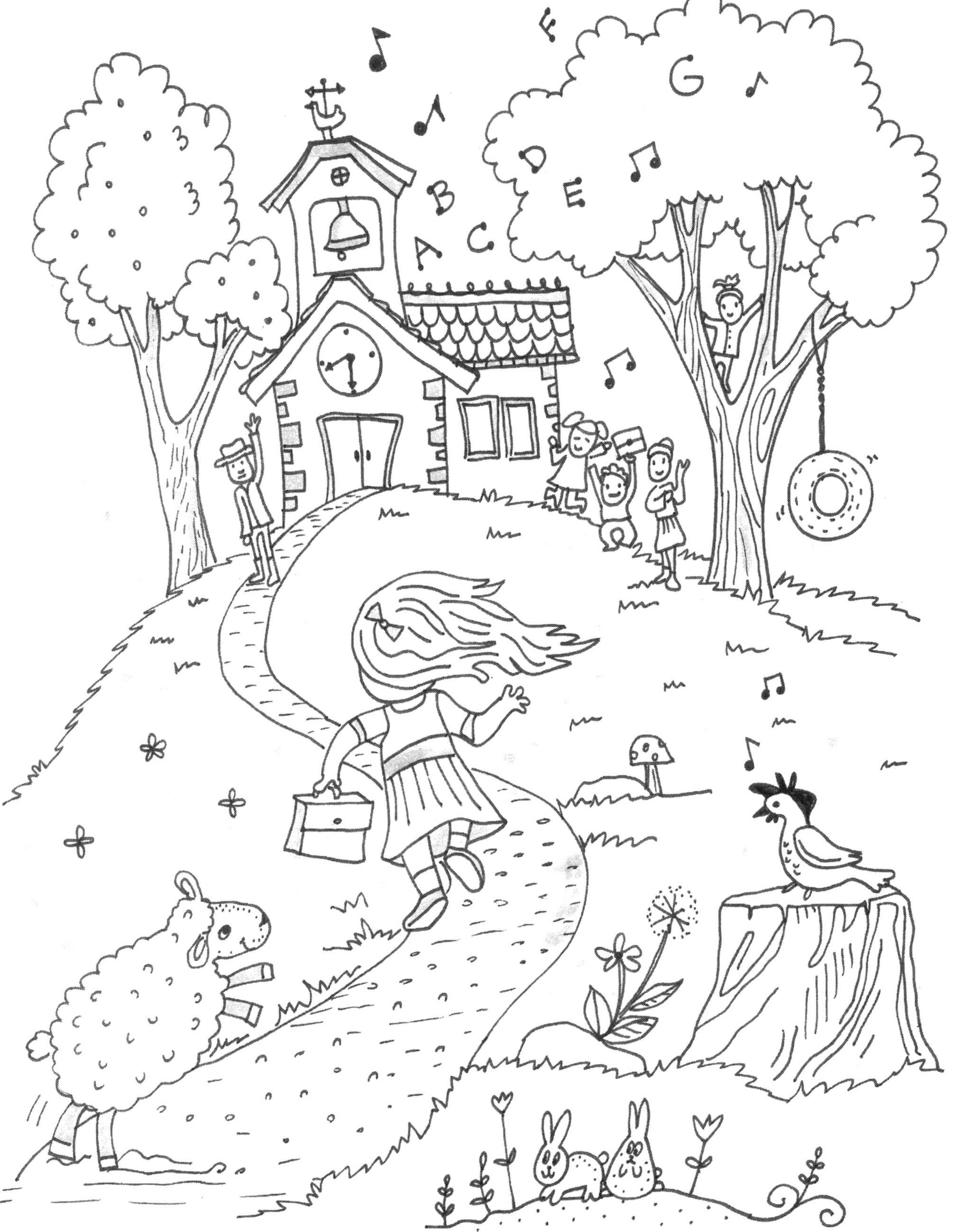
A
B
C
D
E
F
G

SING THE SOUNDS

MARY HAD A LITTLE LAMB

Mary had a little lamb,

Little lamb, little lamb,

Mary had a little lamb,

Its fleece was white at snow.

— Hale, Roulstone, Mason

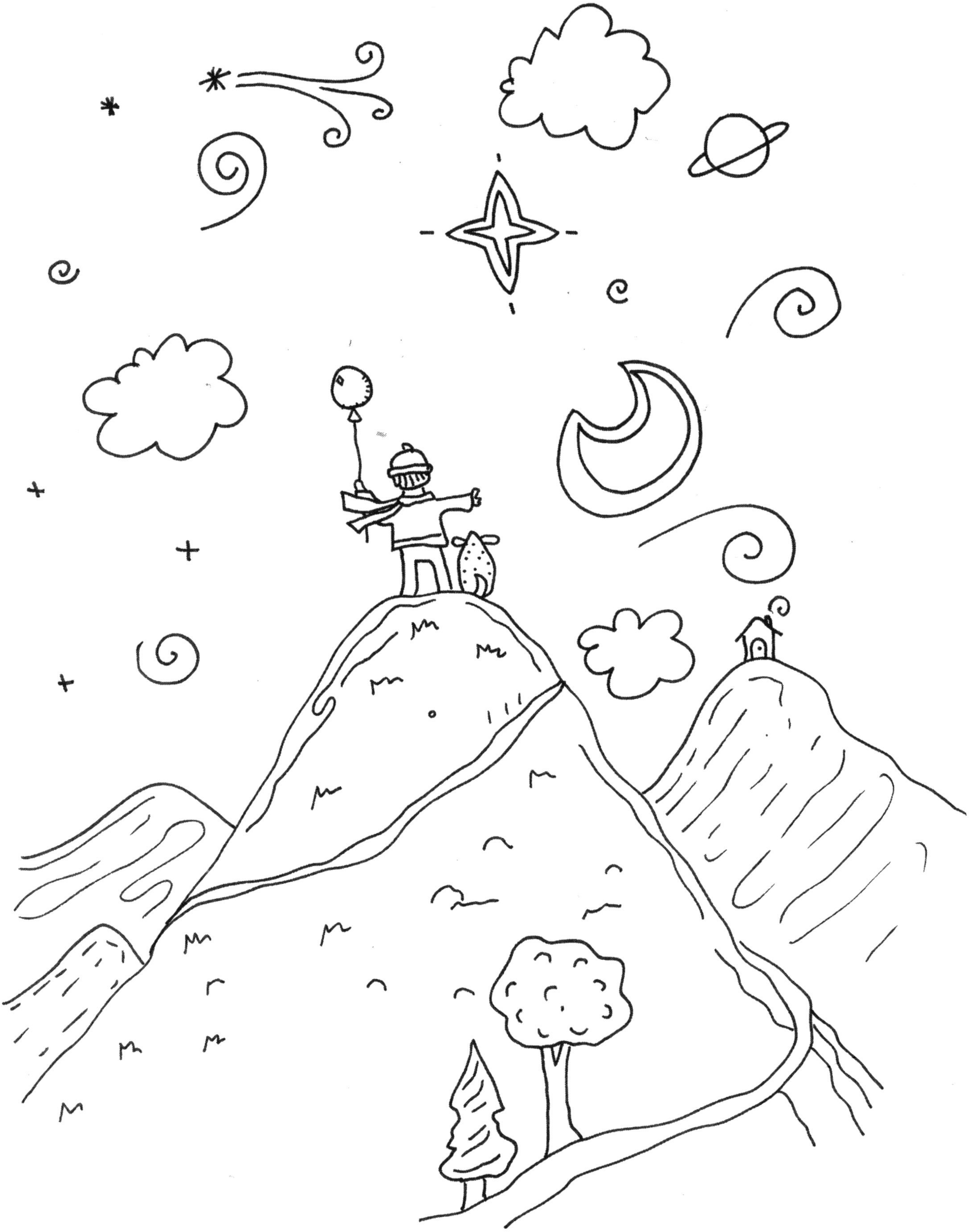

SING THE SOUNDS

TWINKLE, TWINKLE, LITTLE STAR

Twinkle, twinkle, little star,

How I wonder what you are!

Up above the world so high,

Like a diamond in the sky.

Twinkle, twinkle, little star,

How I wonder what you are!

— Jane Taylor

WHAT MAKES A PIANO SOUND?

Open the lid...

STRINGS!

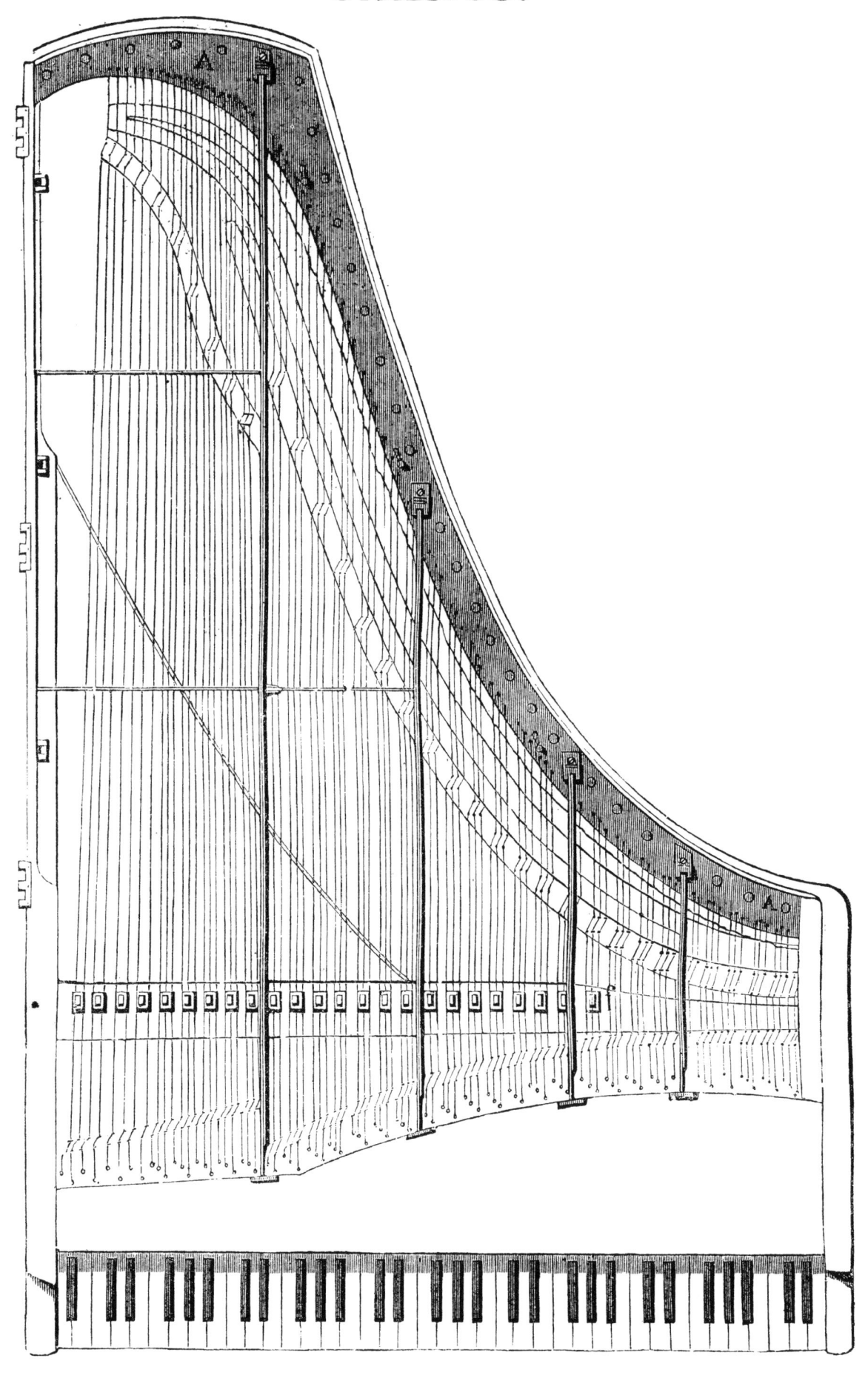

Long + Thick   Short + Thin

=   =

Low Notes   High Notes

Do you see a pattern in the keys?

Circle all the 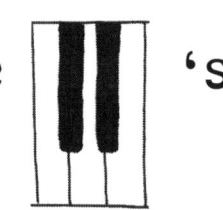 ▮▮'s

Play all the ▮▮'s going

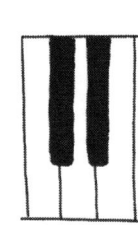

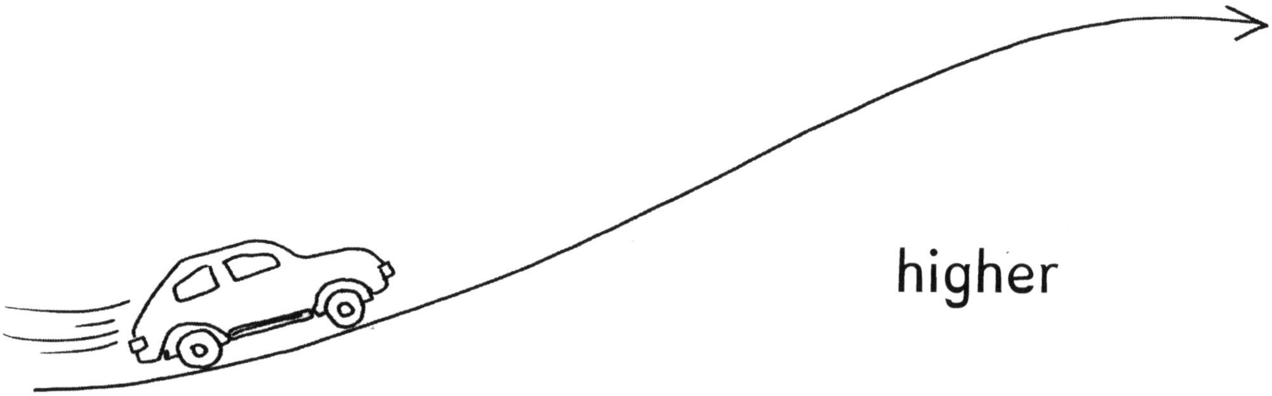

higher

Color the animals that make a high sound.

Do you see <u>another</u> pattern in the keys?

Circle all the [🎹] 's

Play all the [🎹] 's going

lower

Color the animals that make a low sound.

Find your LONGEST finger.

This is finger #3.

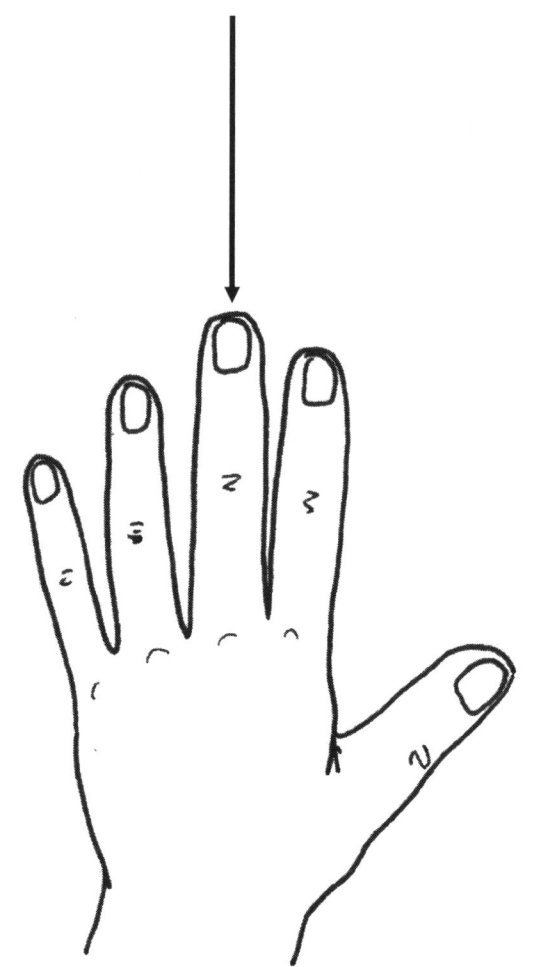

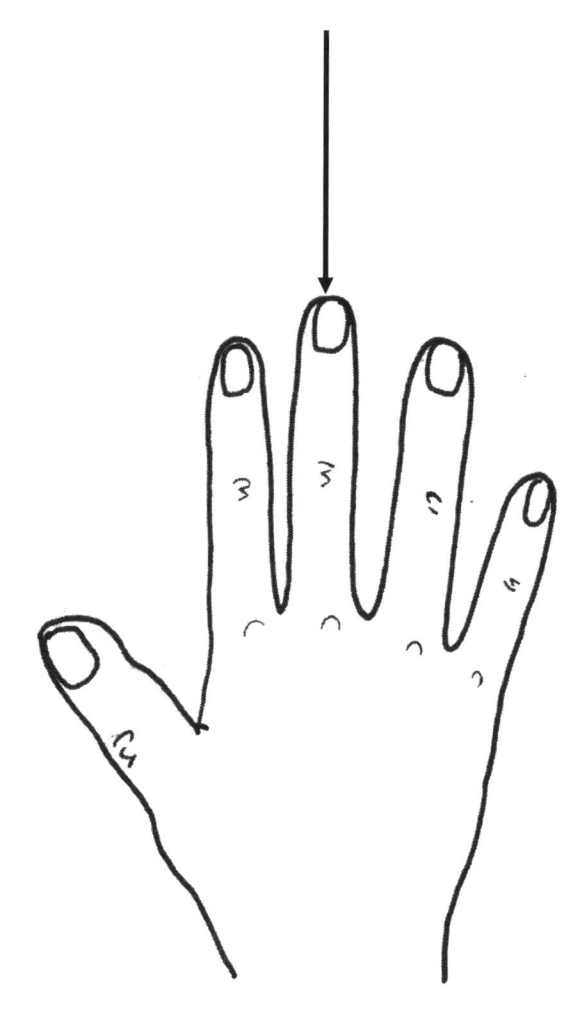

Draw a **LEFT** and **RIGHT** hand.

Write a "**3**" on the **LONGEST** fingers.

LEFT　　　　　　　　　　　　　　　　**RIGHT**

Make an "O" shape with your "3" finger and thumb.

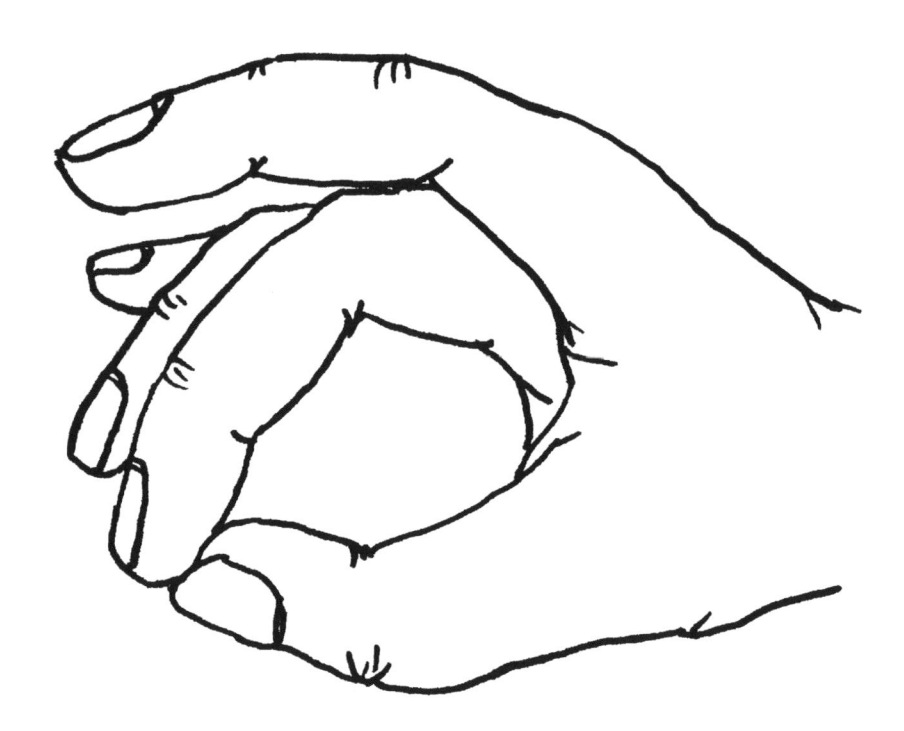

This keeps your "3" finger strong.

With your "3" finger, play

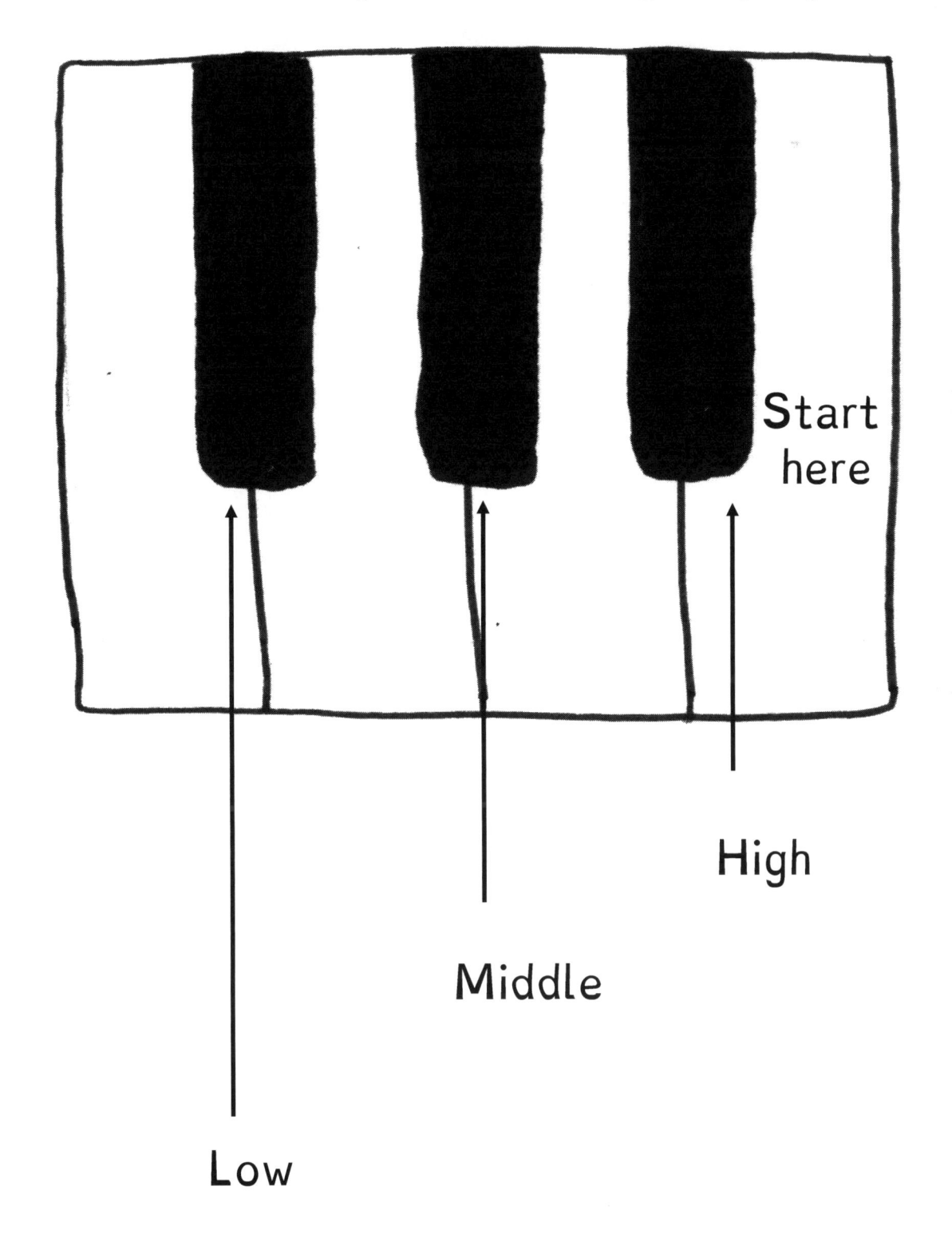

Start here

High

Middle

Low

Make up your own song

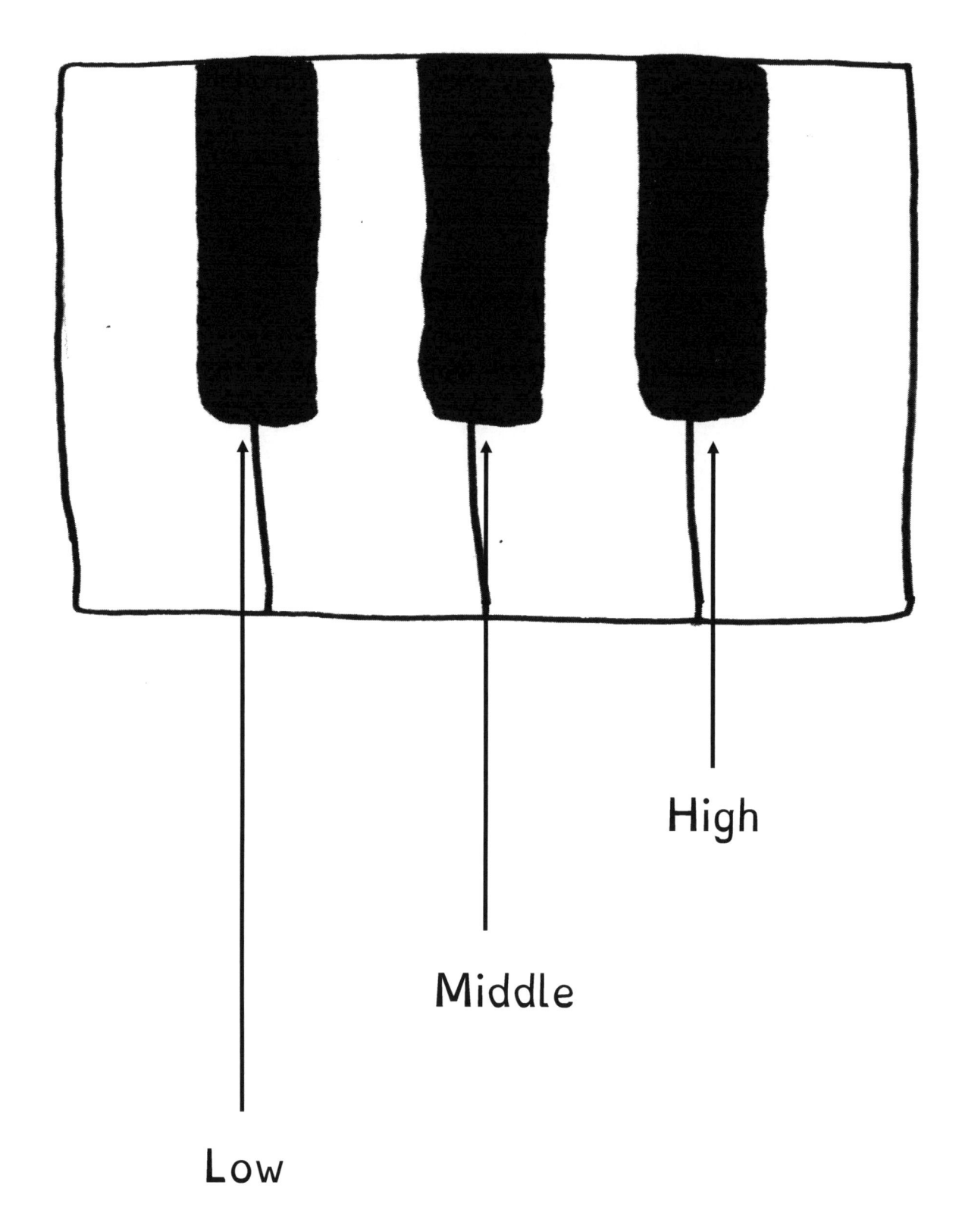

High

Middle

Low

Can you play your song for your mom?

or your dog?

or your friend?

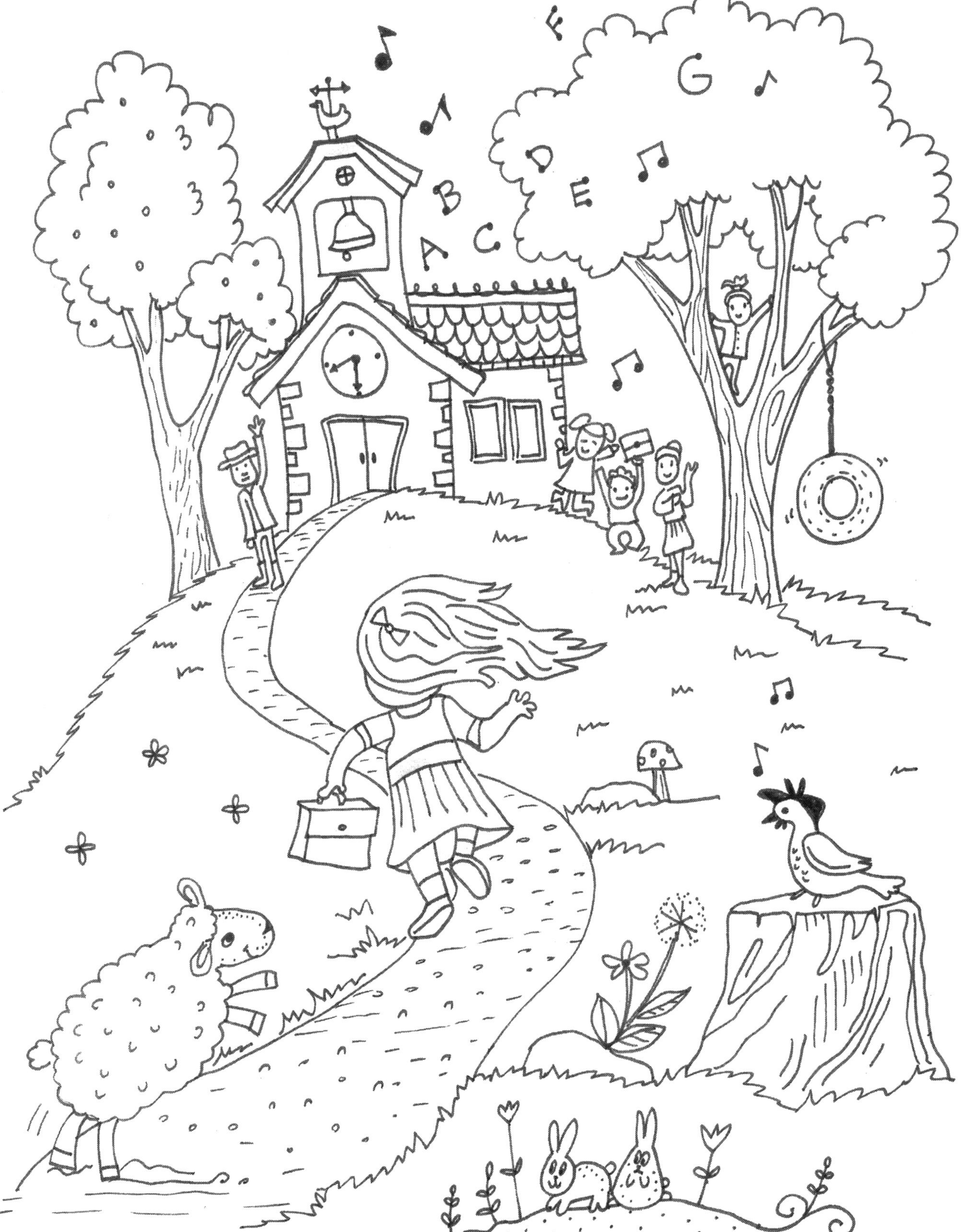

A B C D E F G

What famous song has

HIGH,

MIDDLE,

& LOW

sounds?

MARY HAD A LITTLE LAMB

Starts with

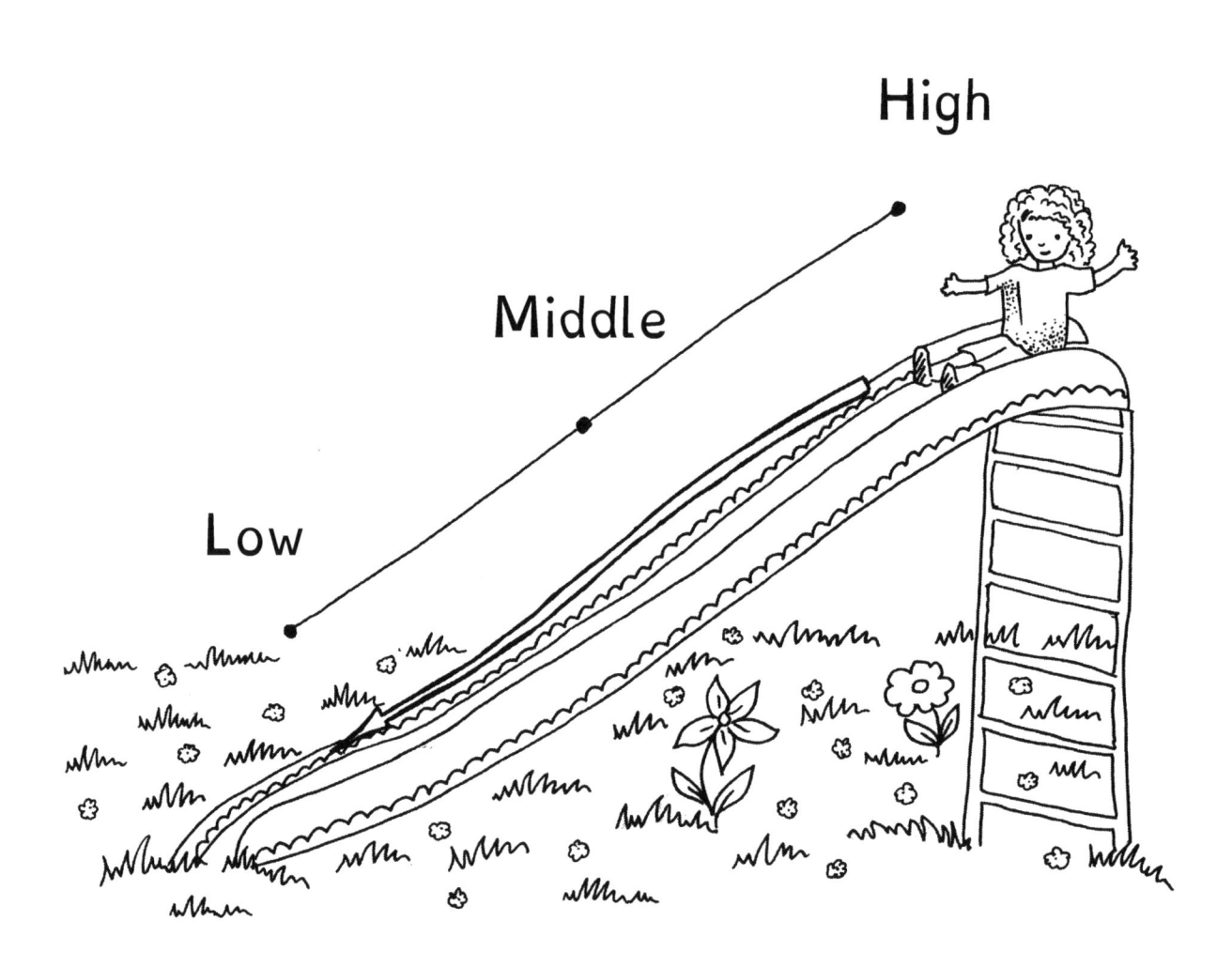

High

Middle

Low

PLAY THIS SONG

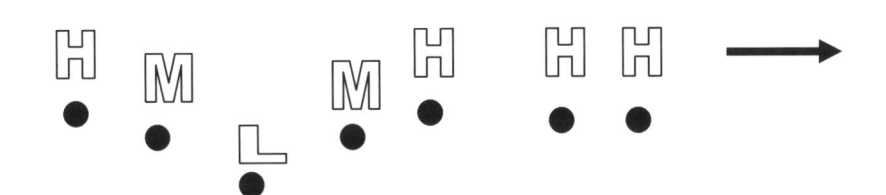

H M L M H H H →

Ma-ry had a lit-tle lamb,

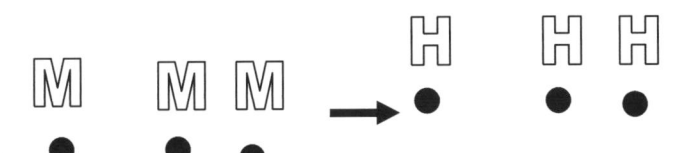

M M M → H H H

Lit-tle lamb, lit-tle lamb,

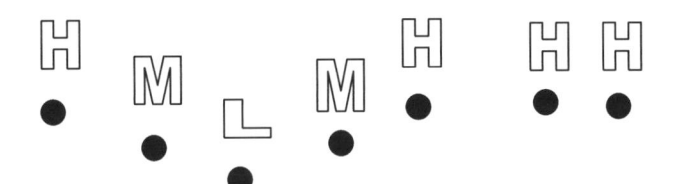

H M L M H H H

Ma-ry had a lit-tle lamb,

H M M H M L →

Its fleece was white at snow

(→ = LONG NOTE)

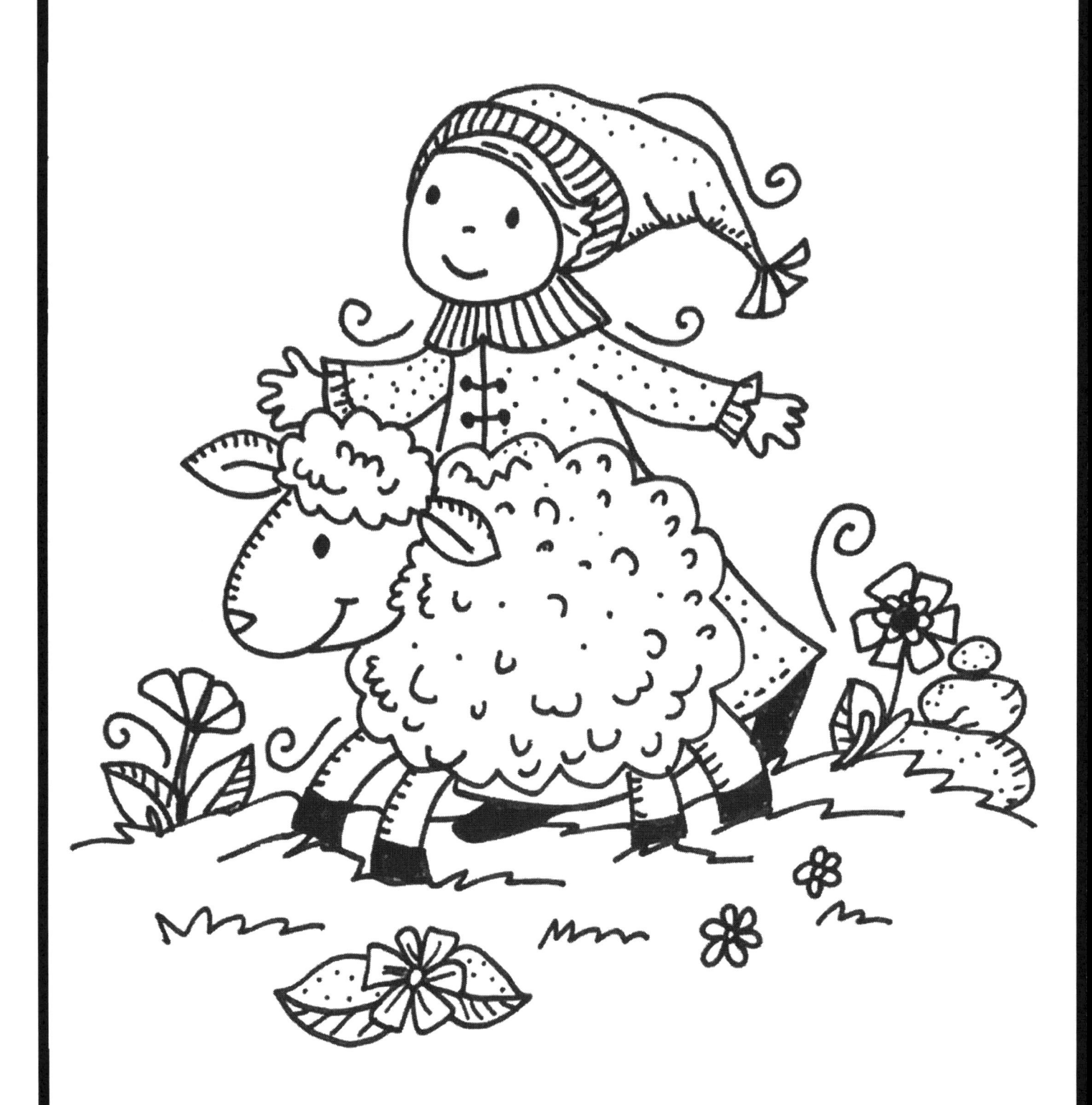

CHALLENGE

Play "Mary Had a Little Lamb" with your "3" fingers from BOTH hands at the SAME time.

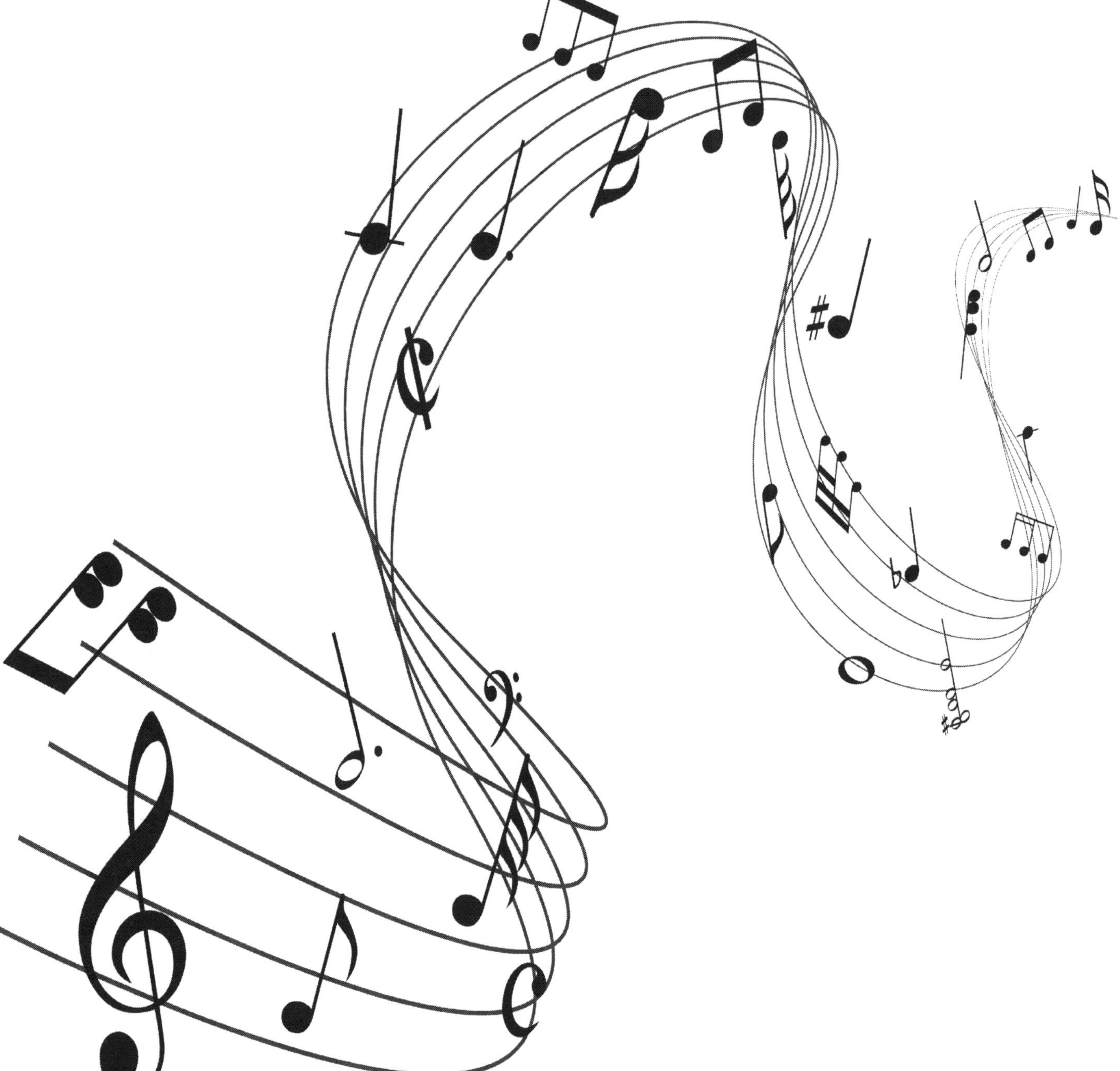

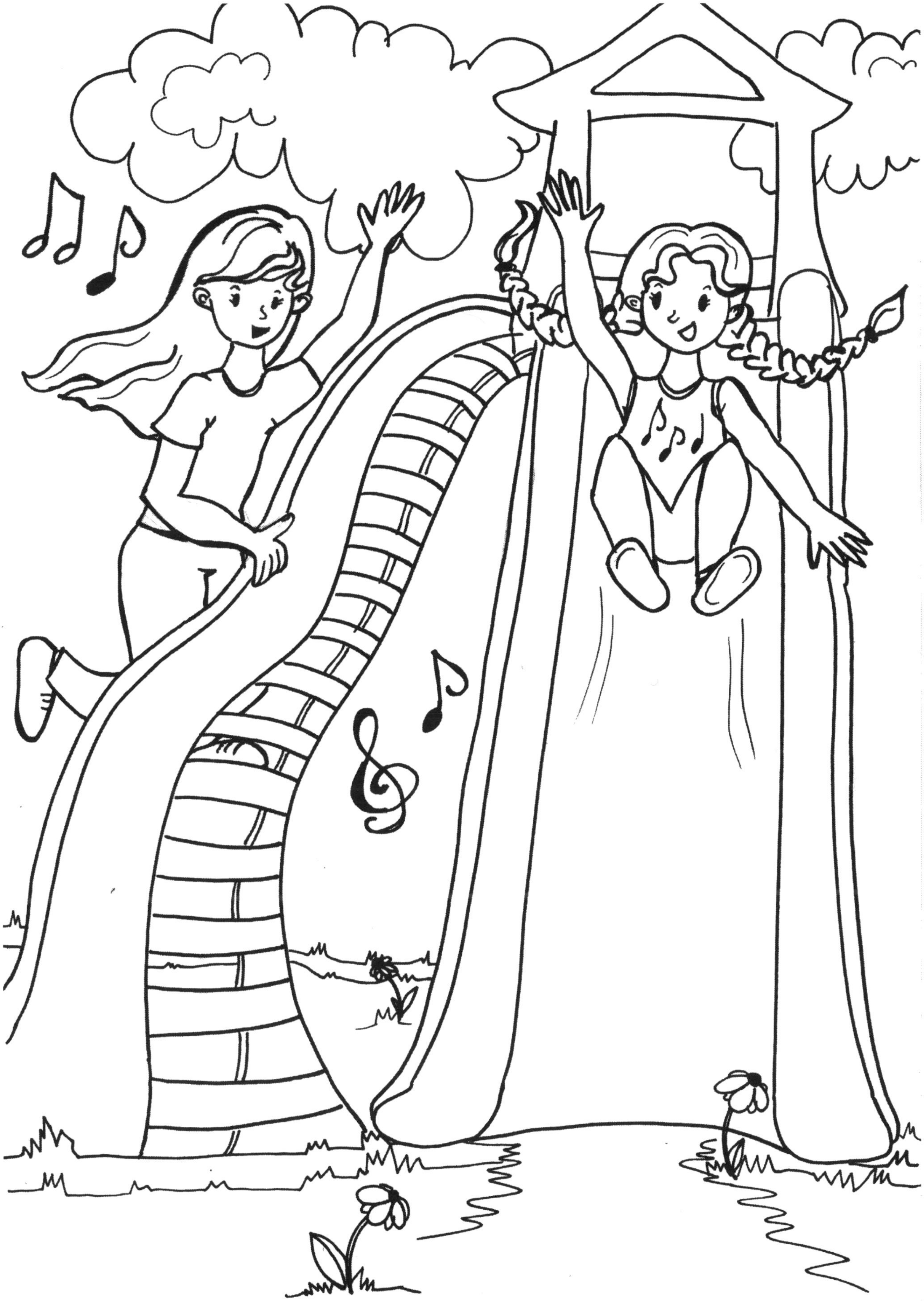

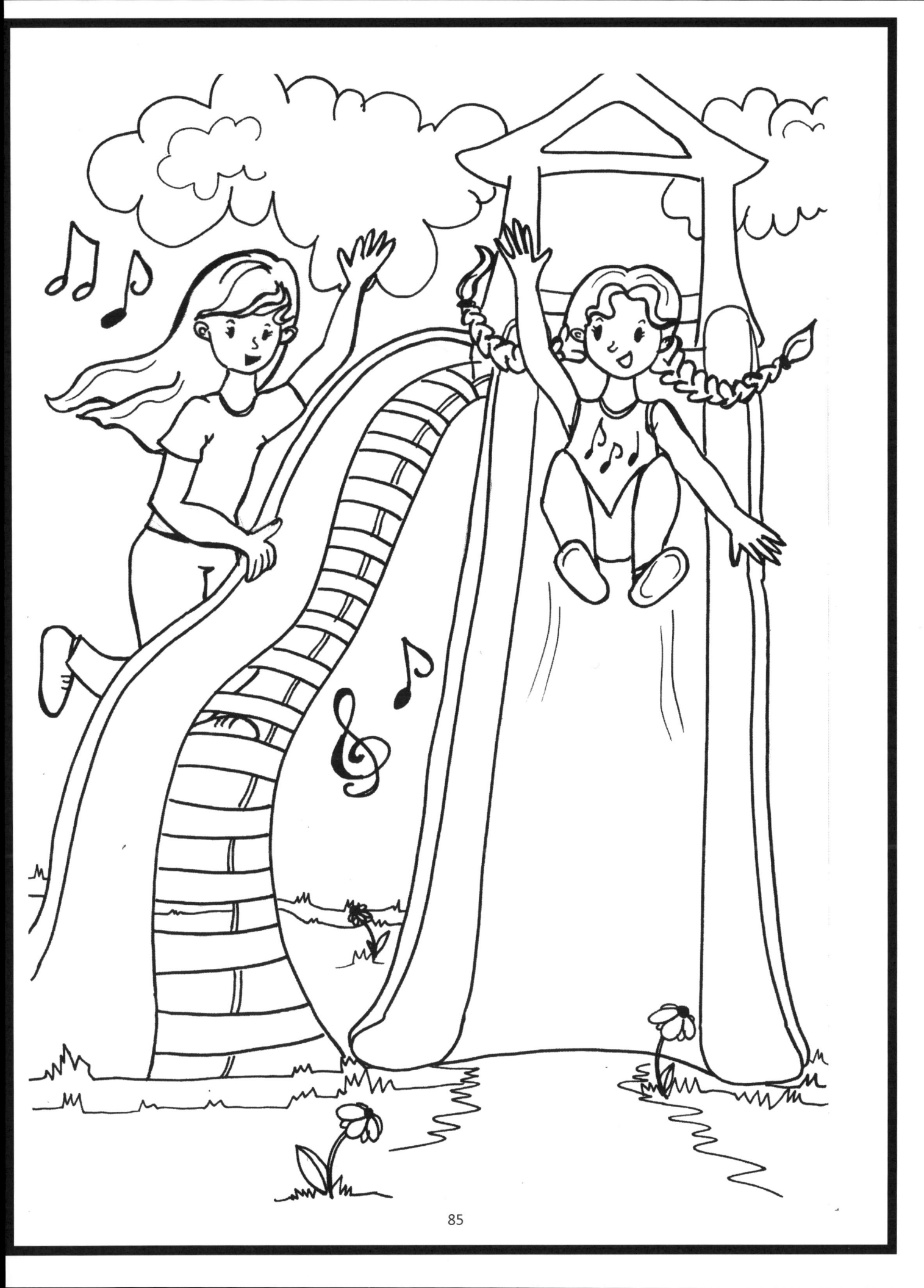

LEFT HAND

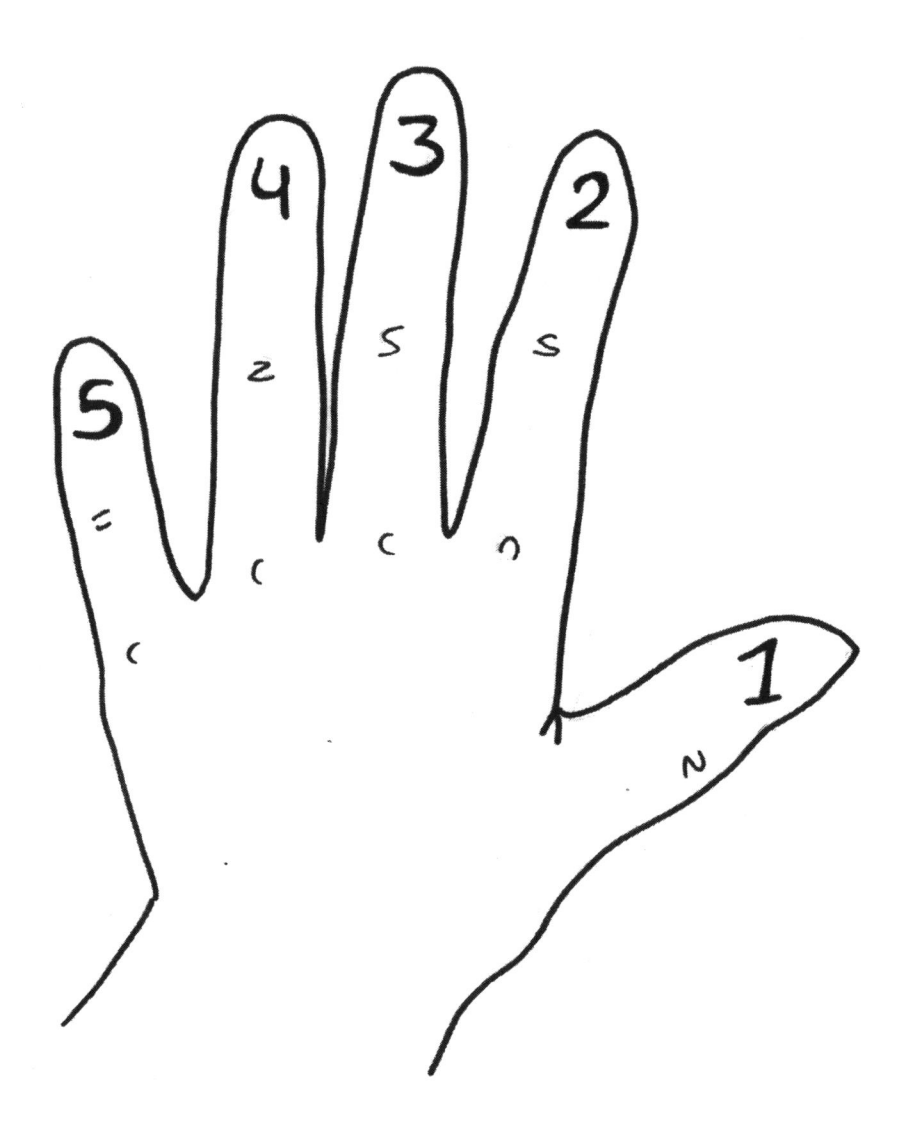

THUMBS are always **1**'s

RIGHT HAND

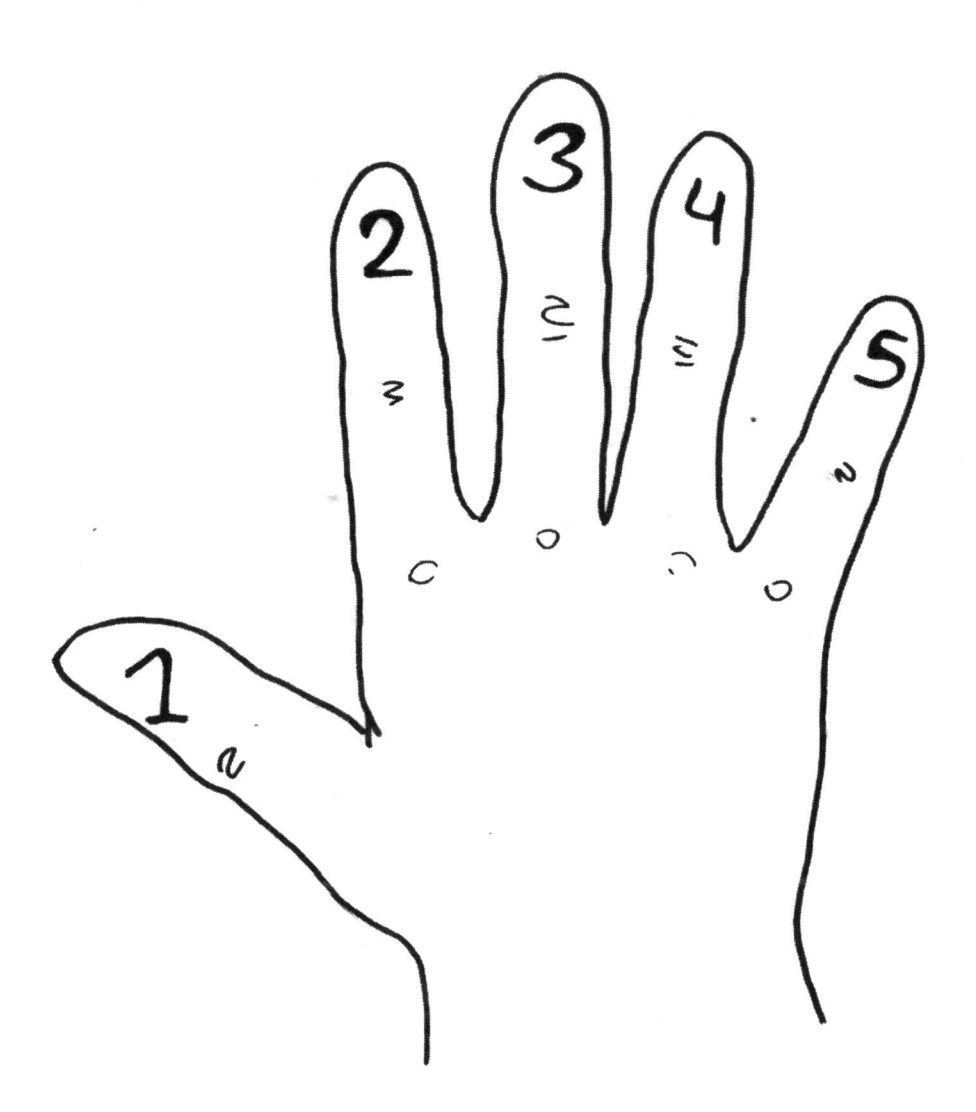

THUMBS are always **1**'s

C C

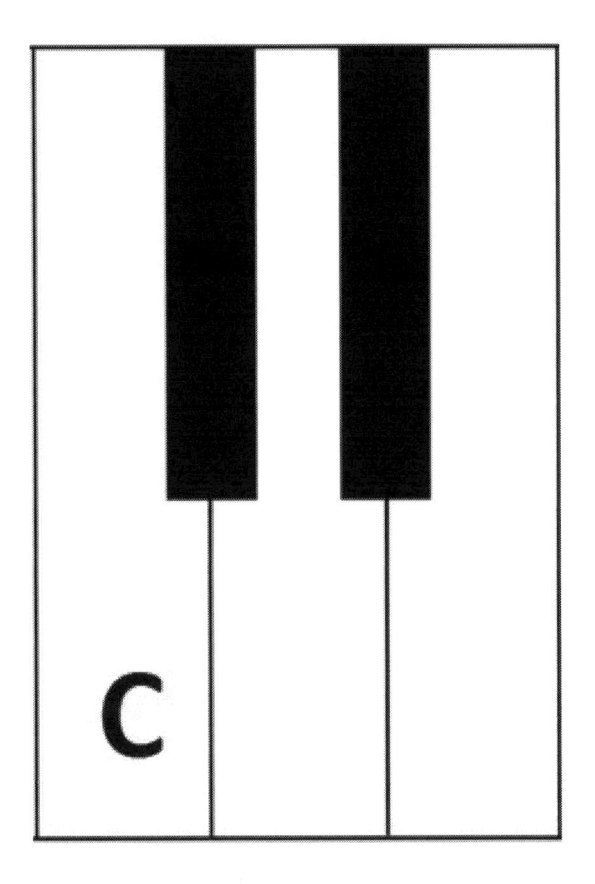

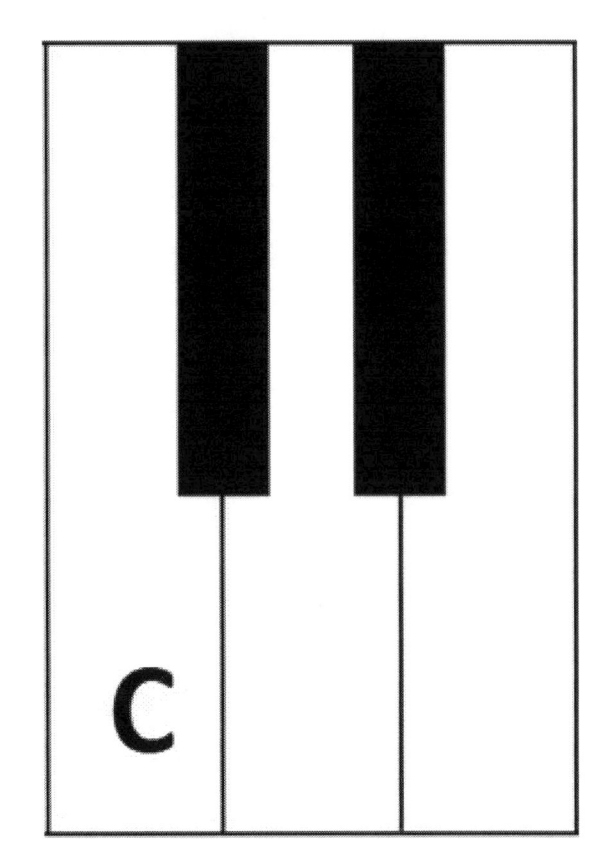

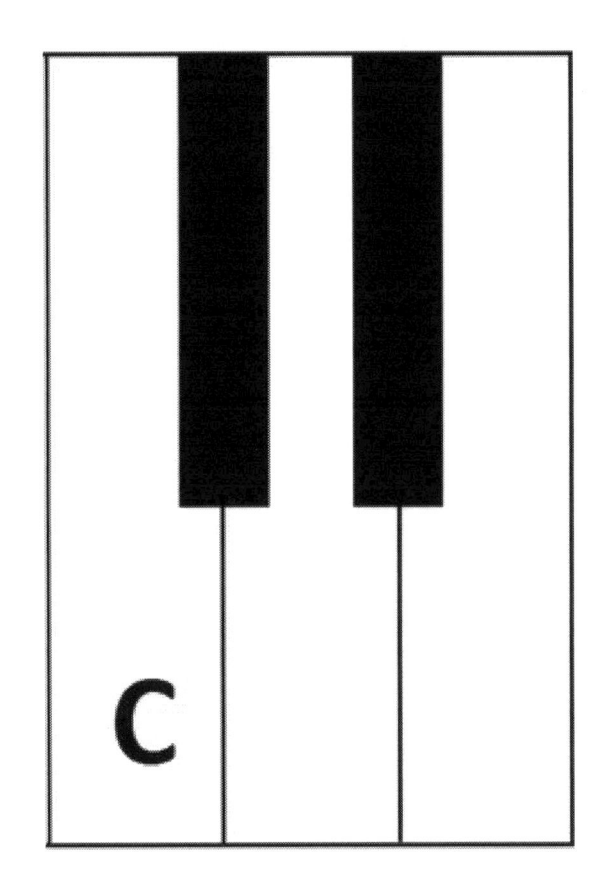

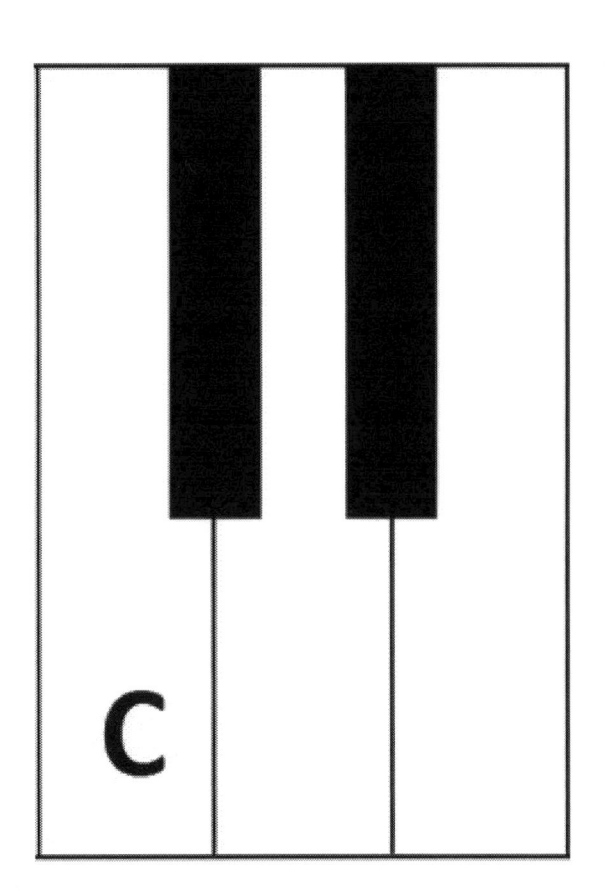

C C

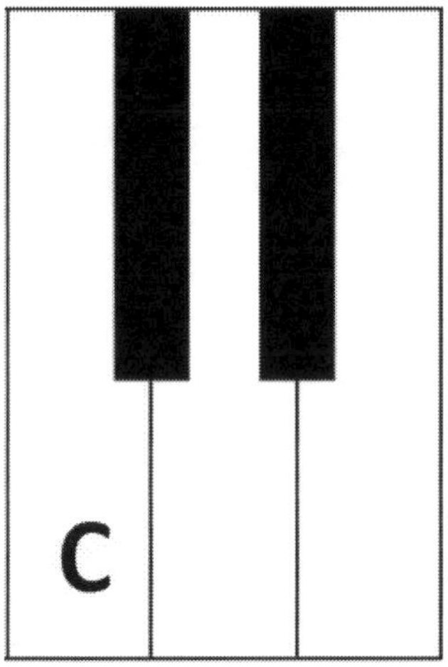
C

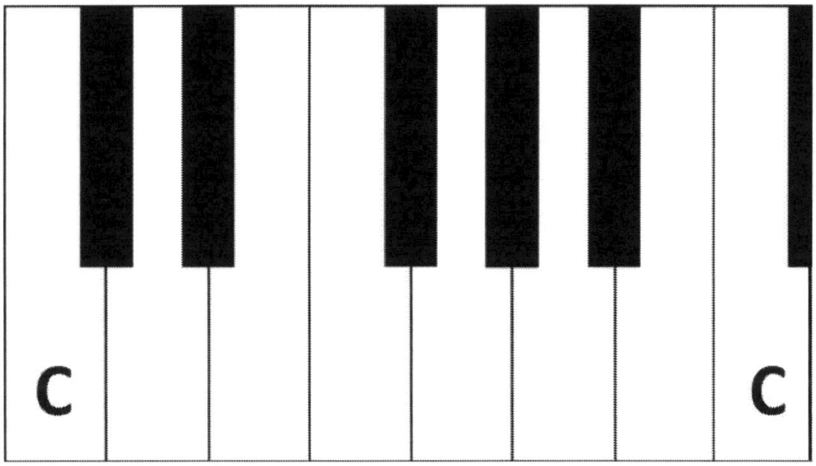
C
C

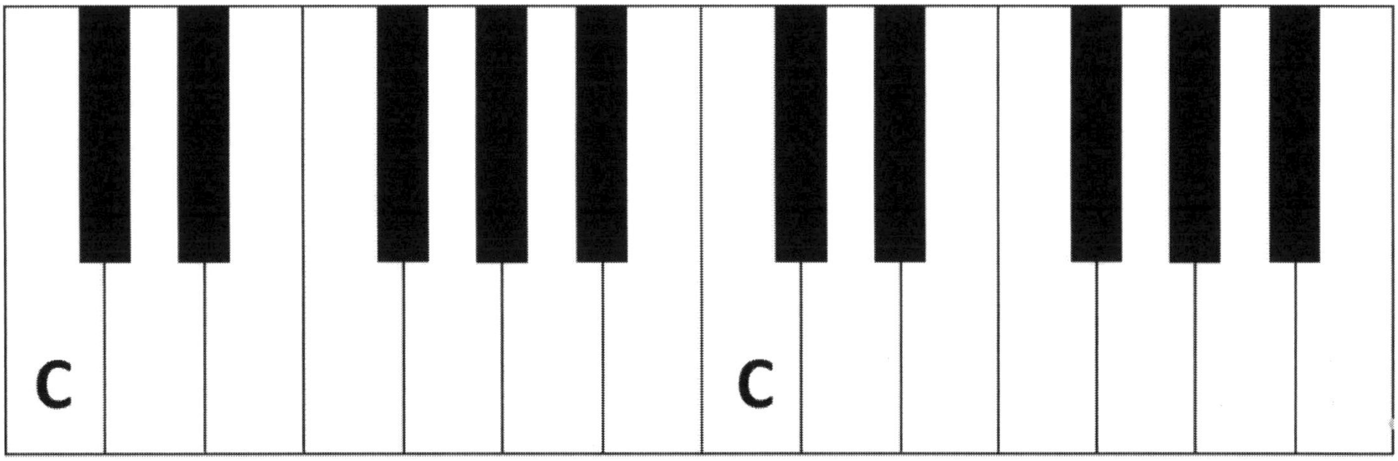
C
C

STEADY BEAT

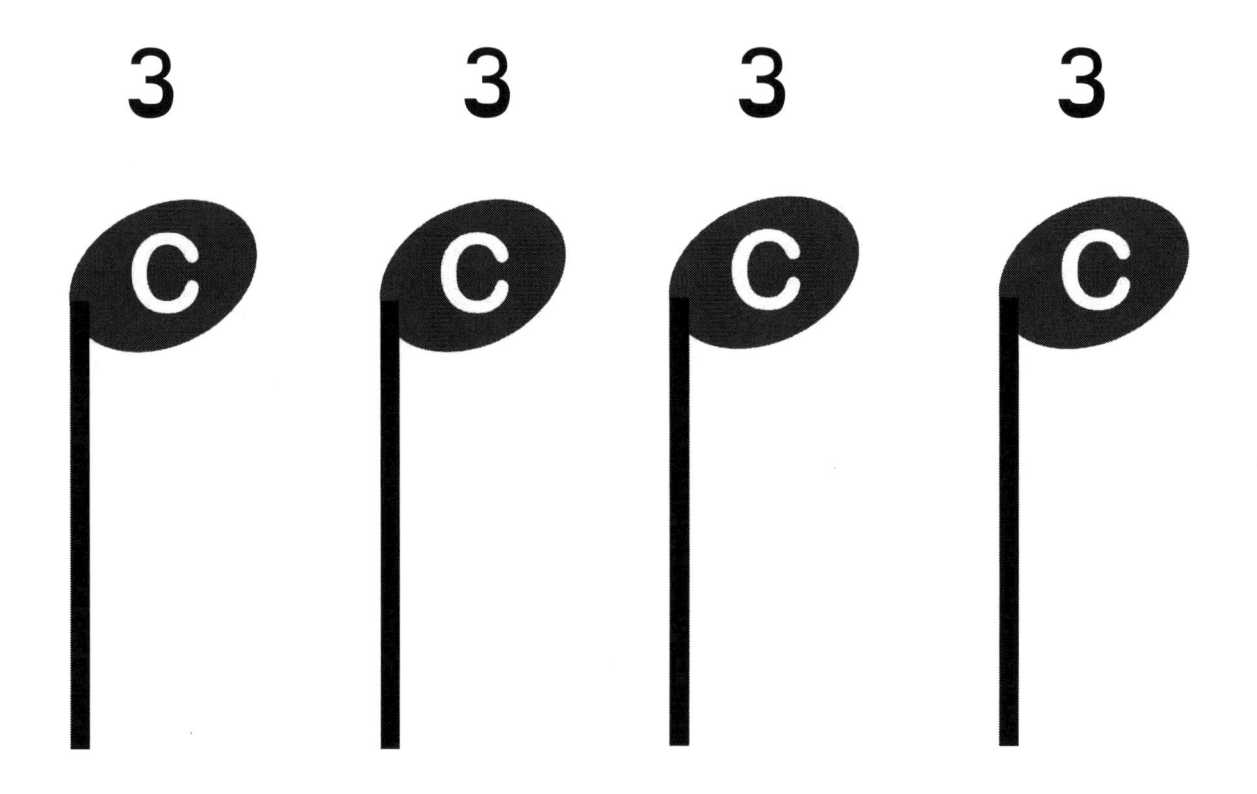

3   **3**   **3**   **3**

C   C   C   C

LEFT HAND (LH)

STEADY BEAT

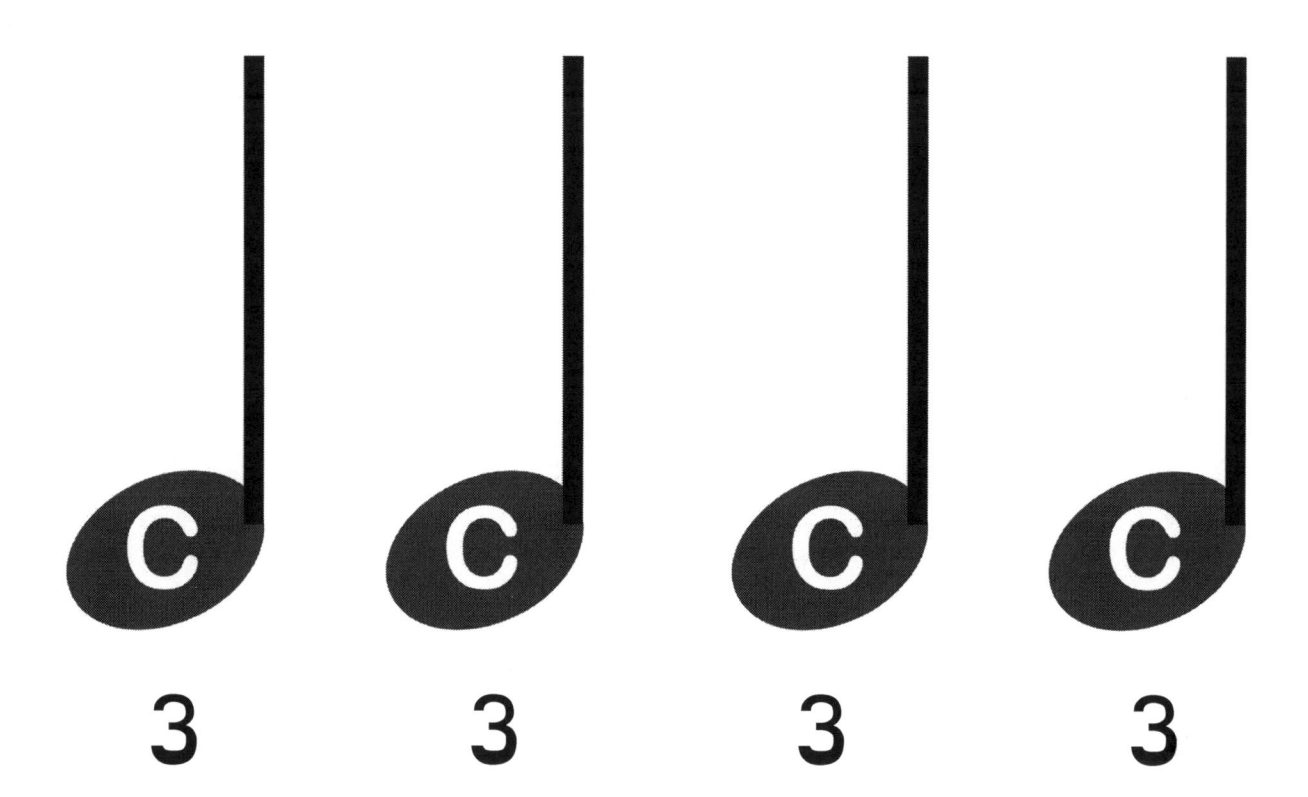

C 3 C 3 C 3 C 3

RIGHT HAND (RH)

BELL CHIMES

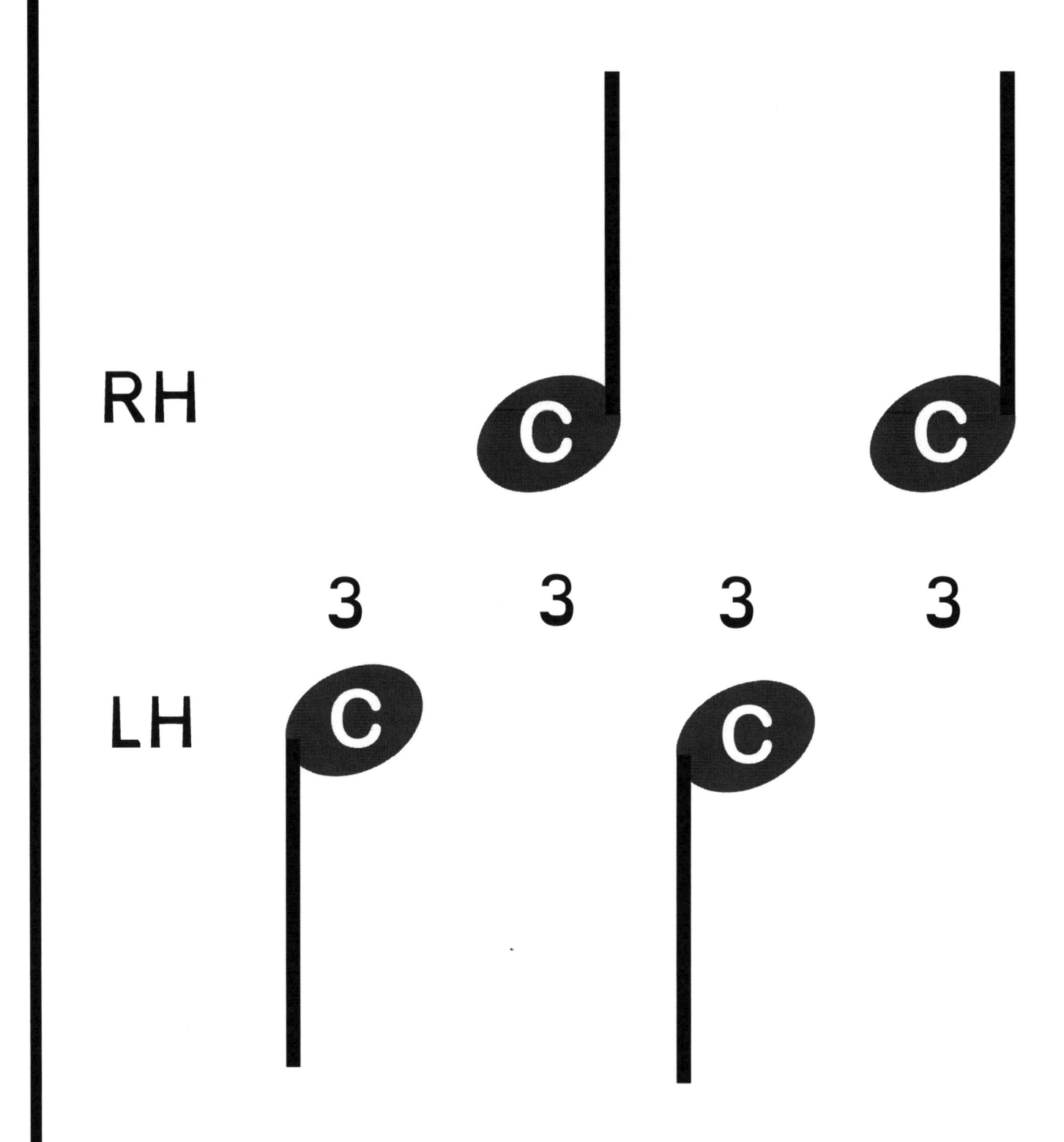

RH

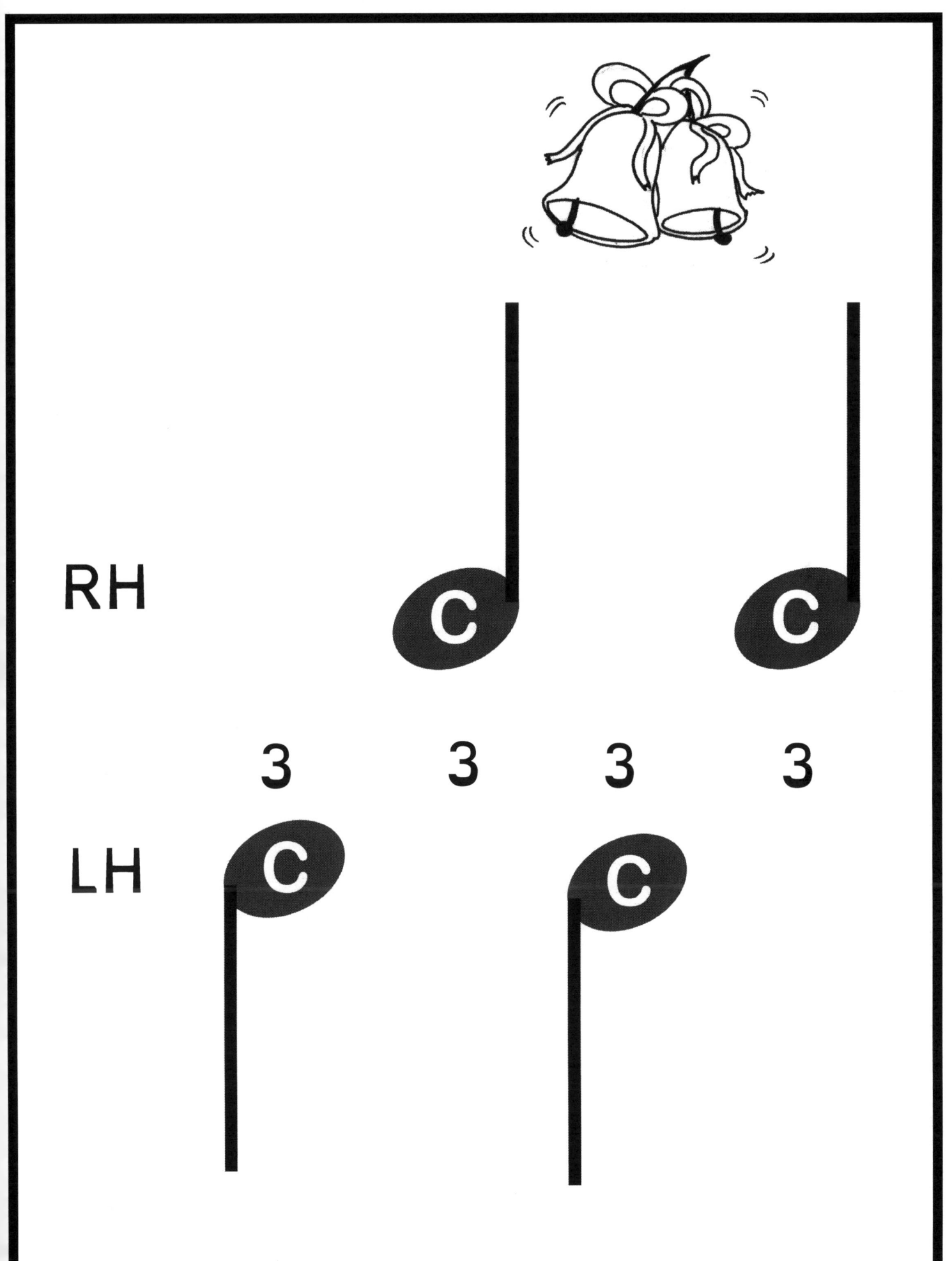

3 3 3 3

LH

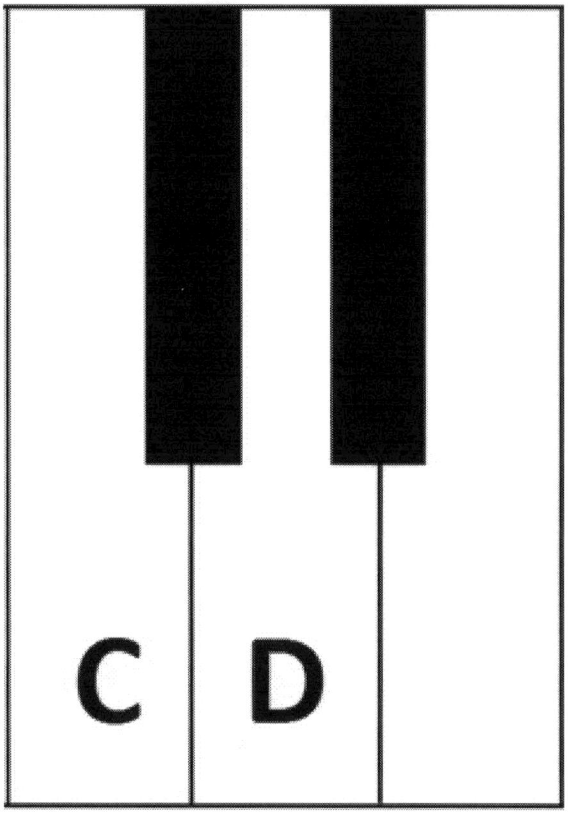
C
D

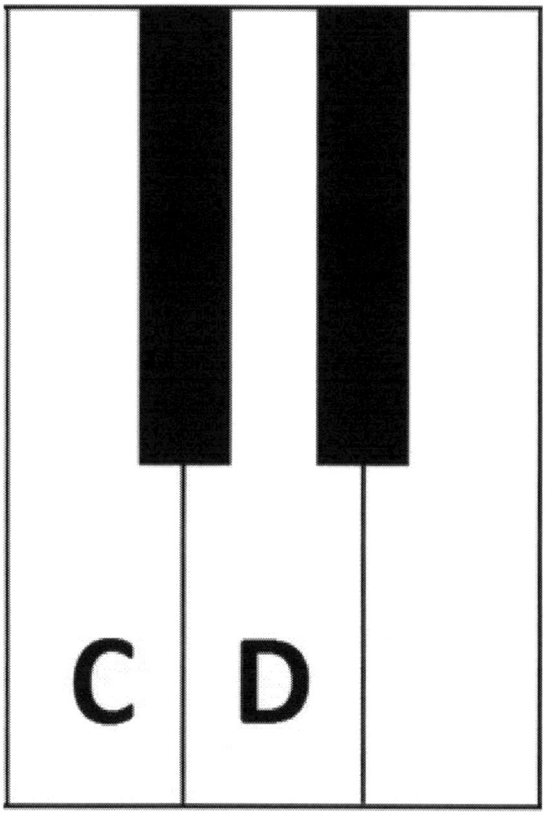
C
D

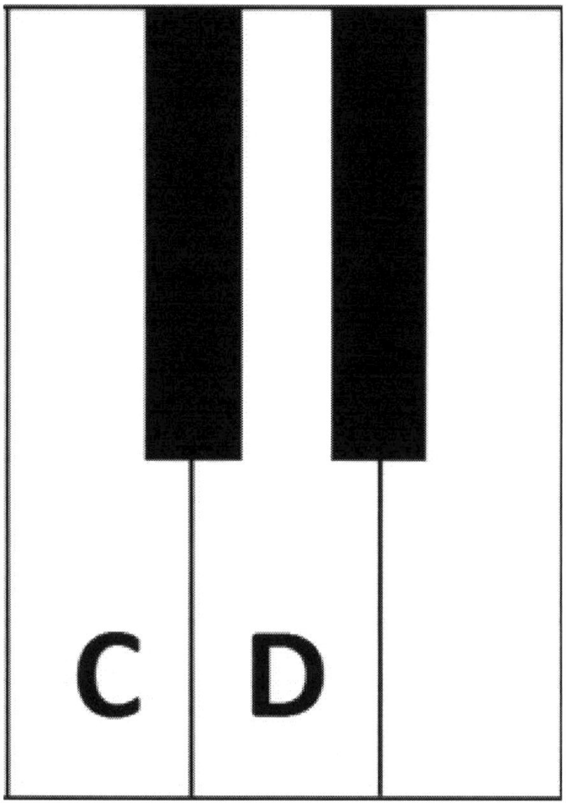
C
D

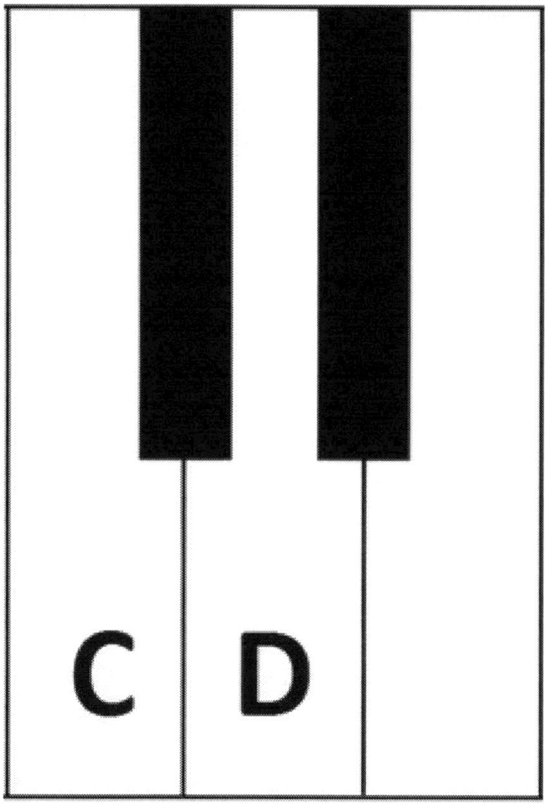
C
D

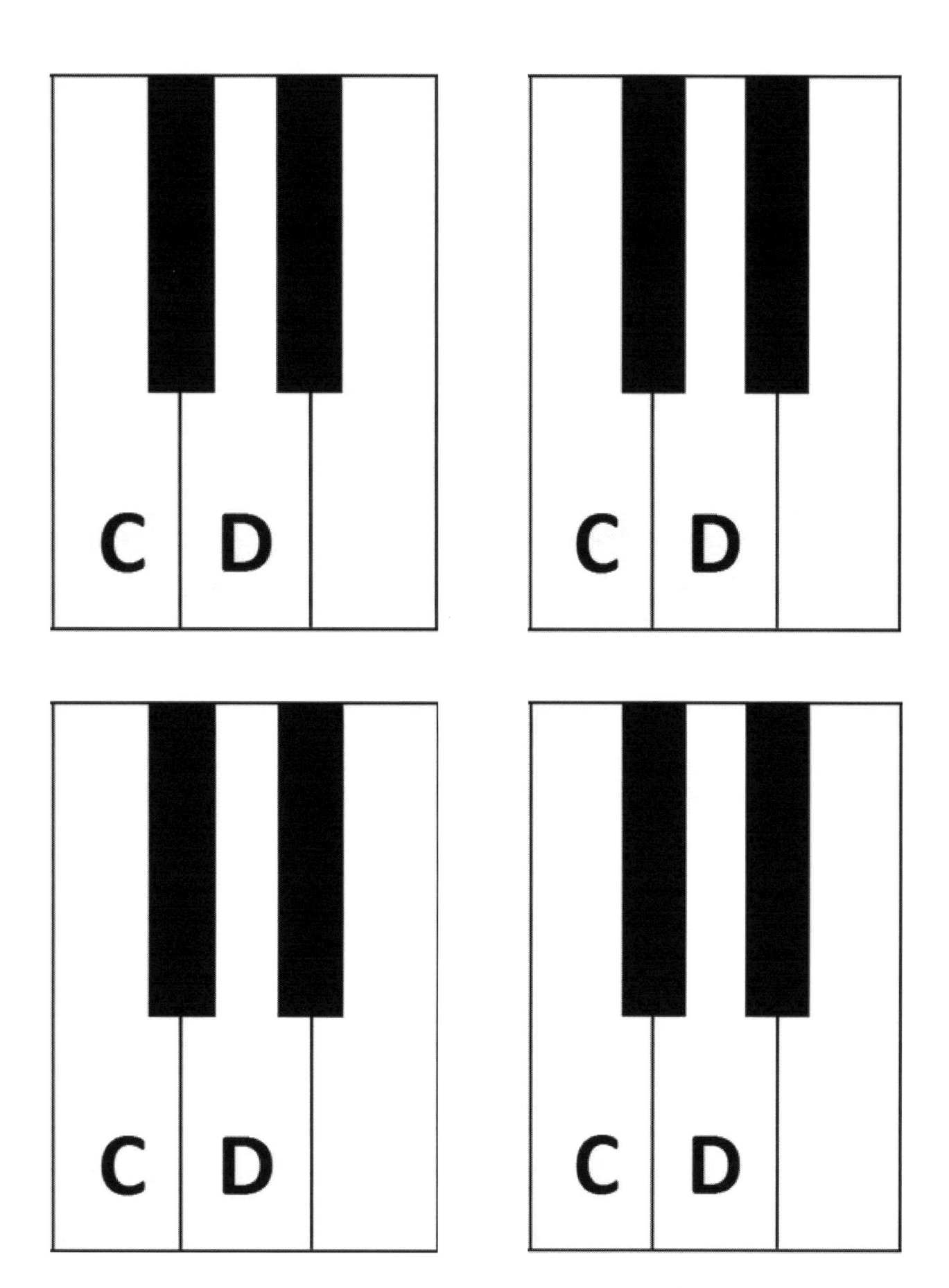

95

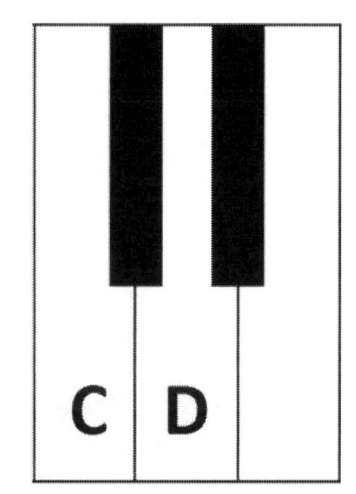

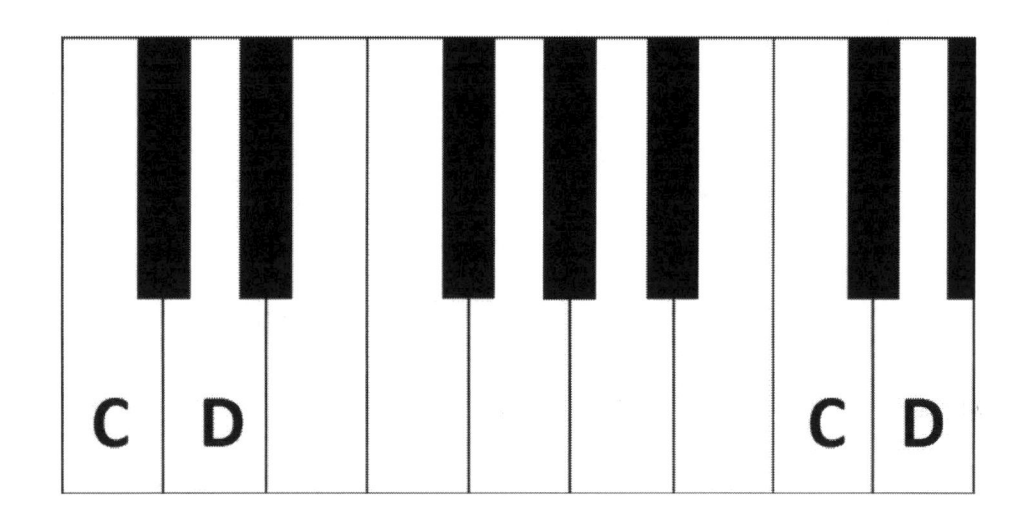

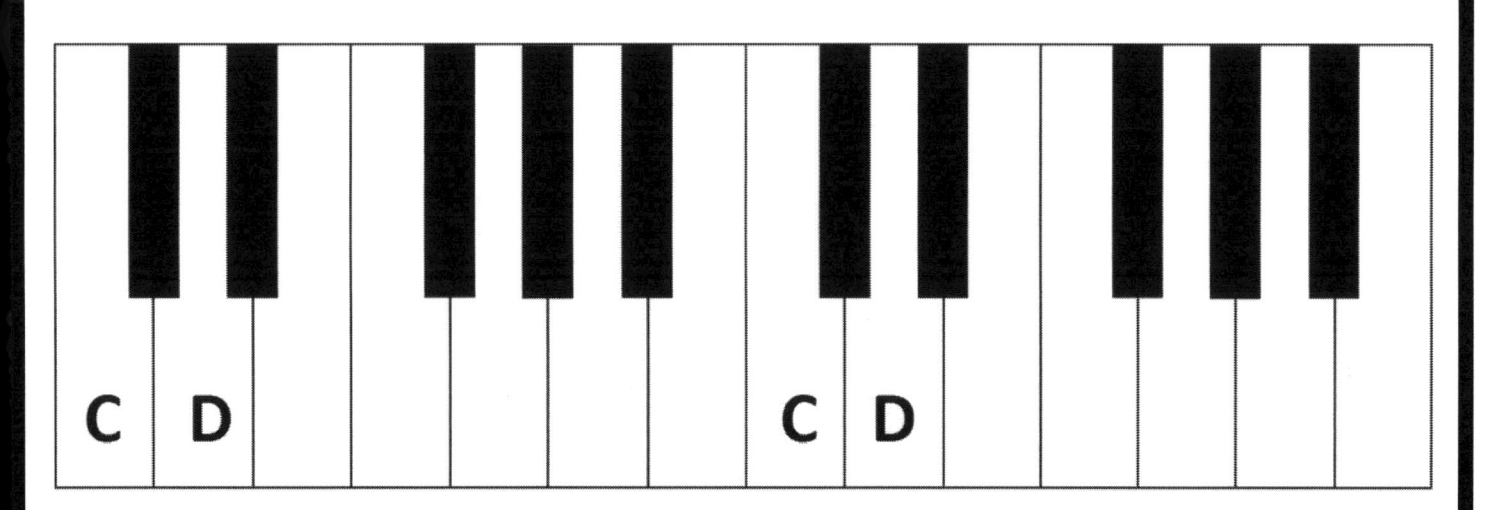

SHARKS

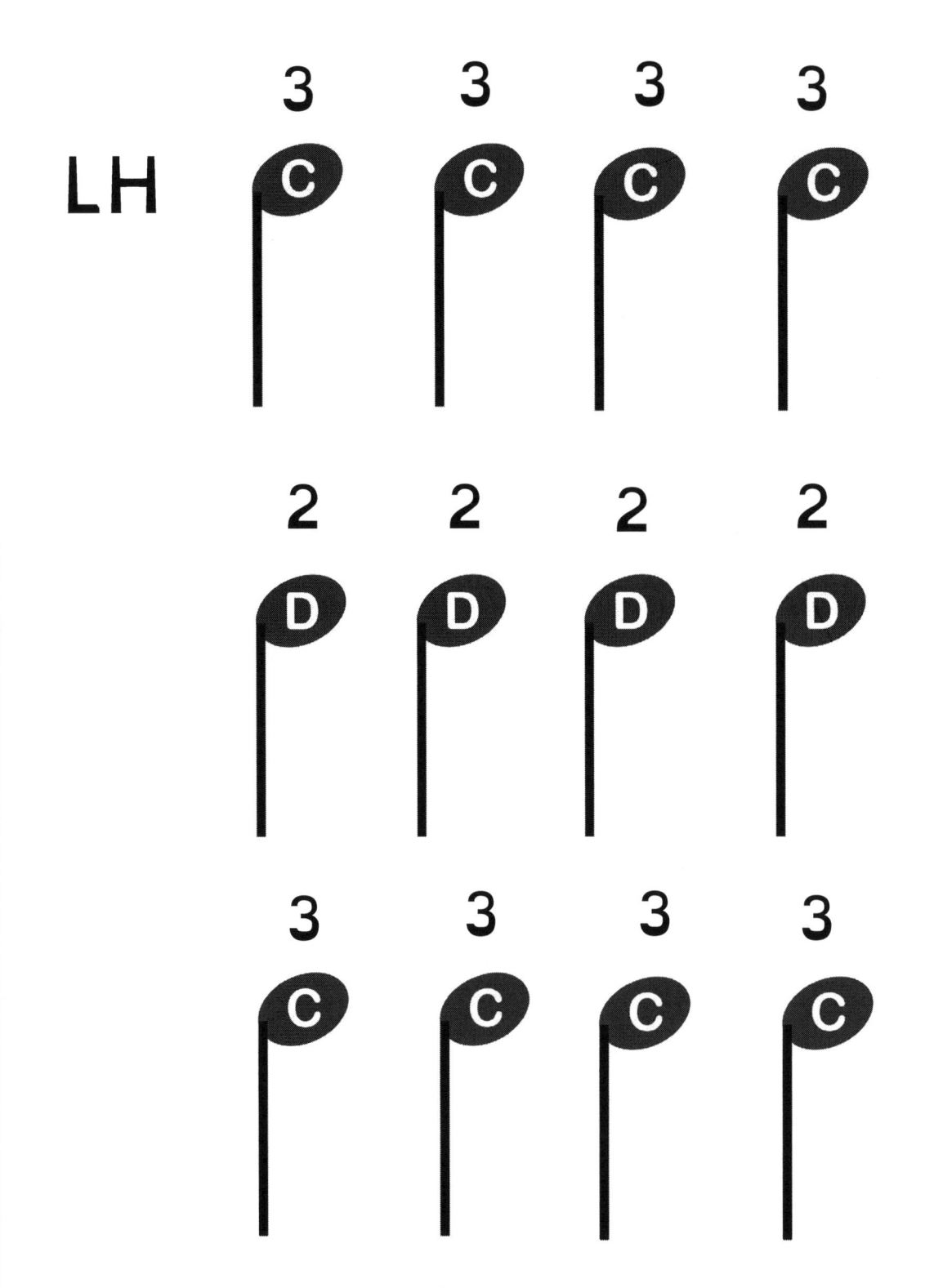

LH 3 3 3 3
    C C C C

    2 2 2 2
    D D D D

    3 3 3 3
    C C C C

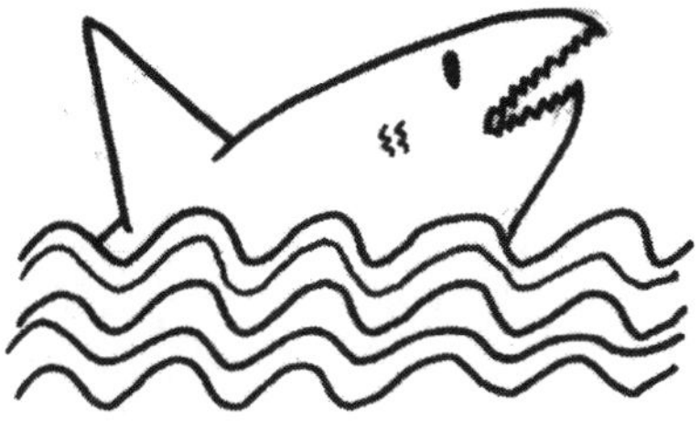

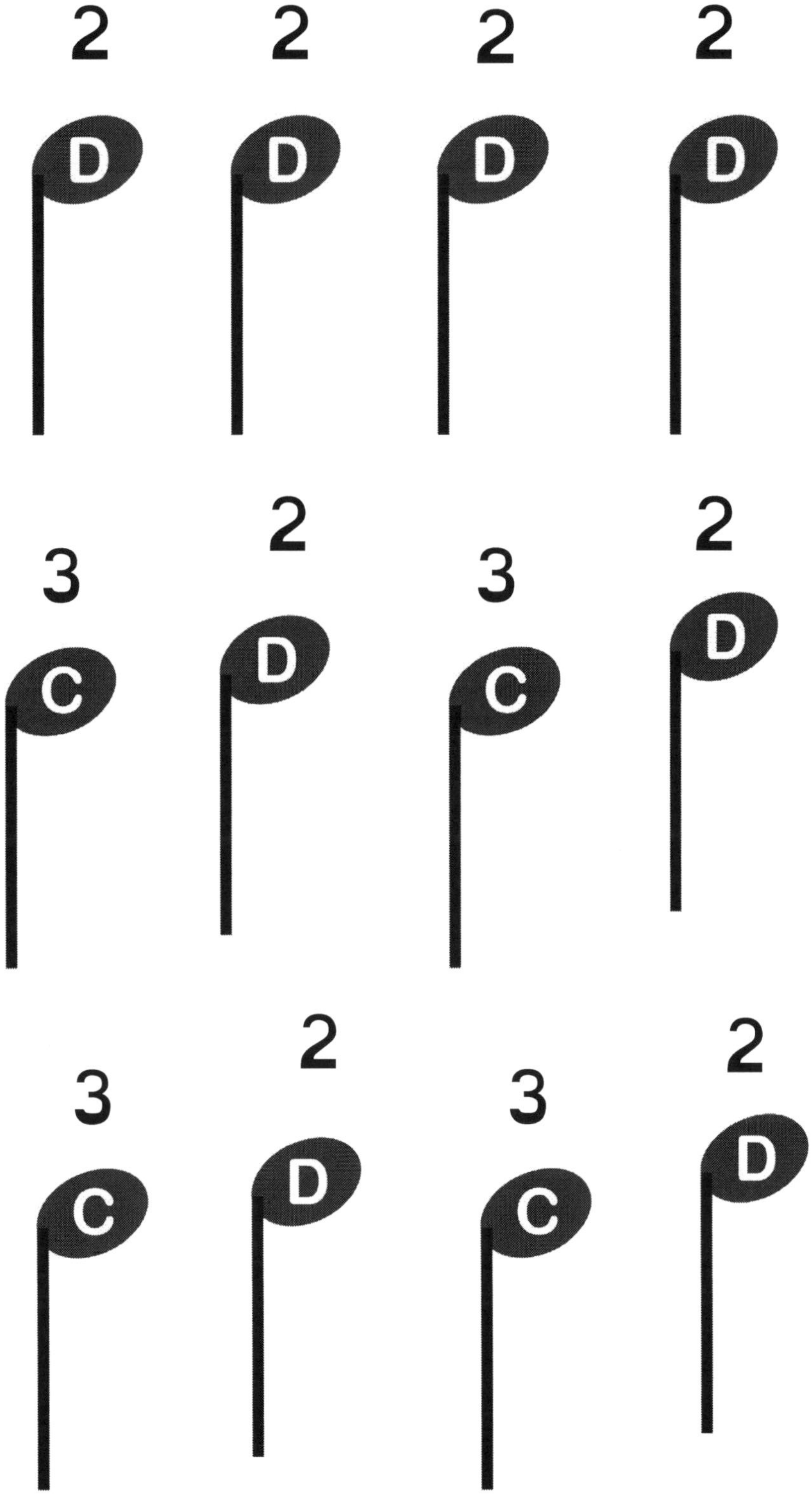
2 2 2 2
D D D D
3 2 3 2
C D C D
3 2 3 2
C D C D

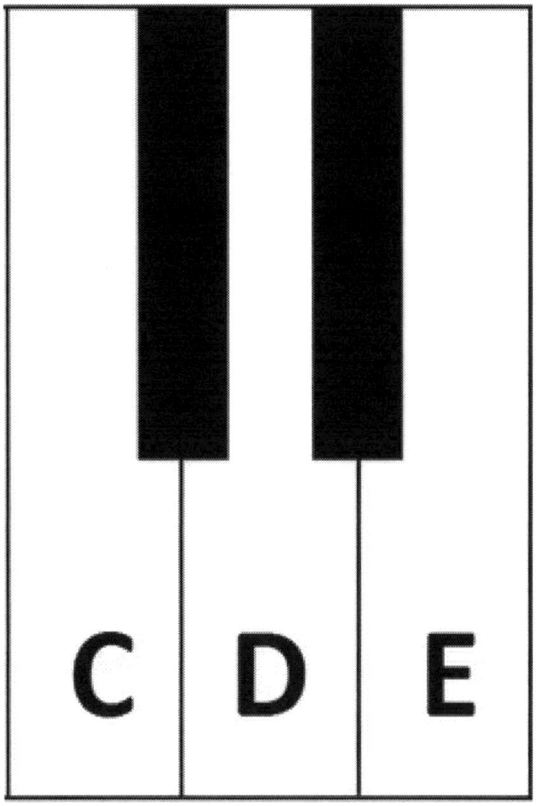
C
D
E

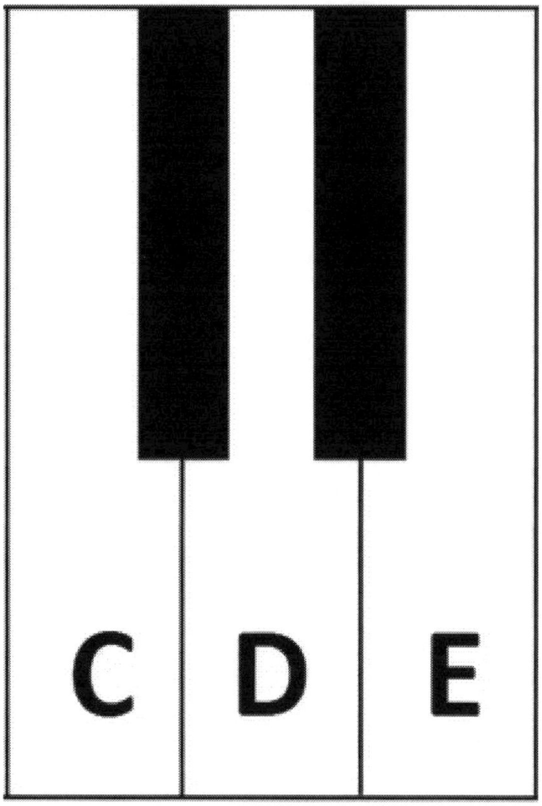
C
D
E

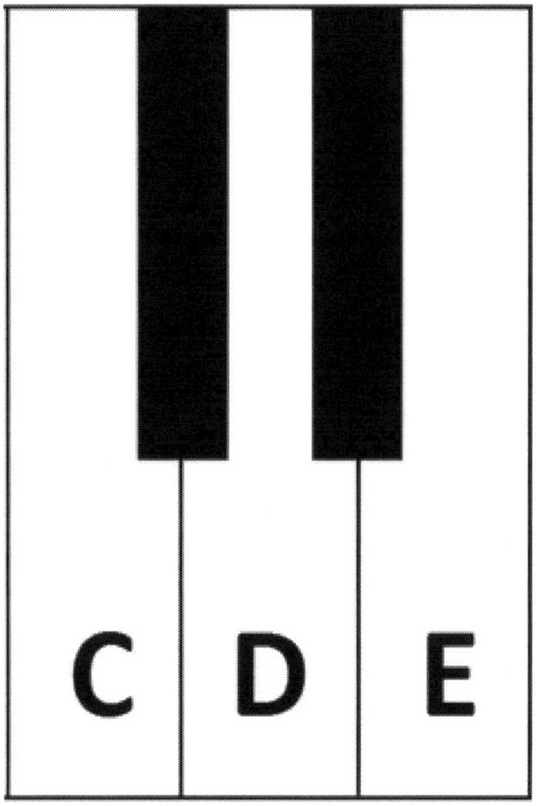
C
D
E

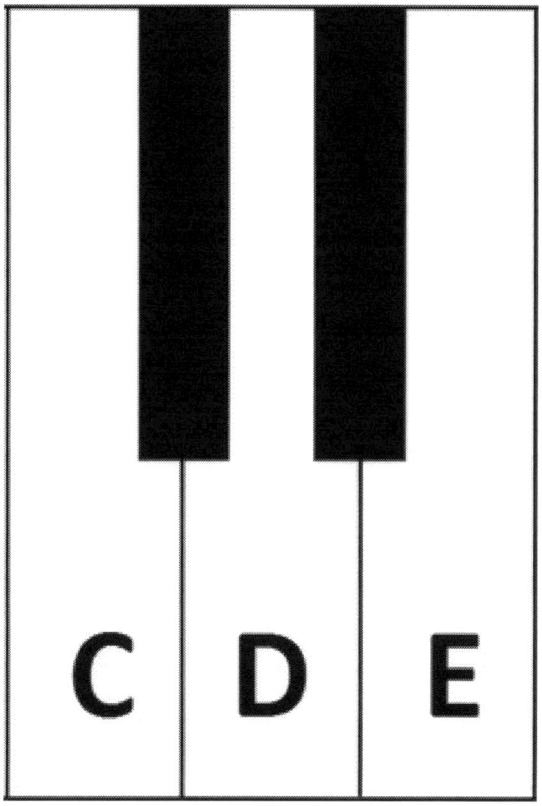
C
D
E

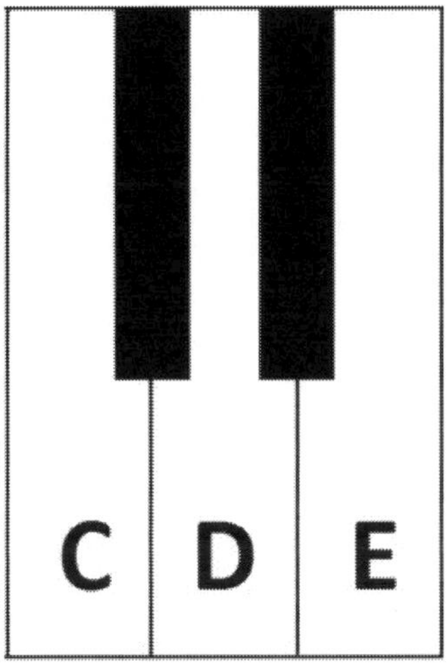
C D E

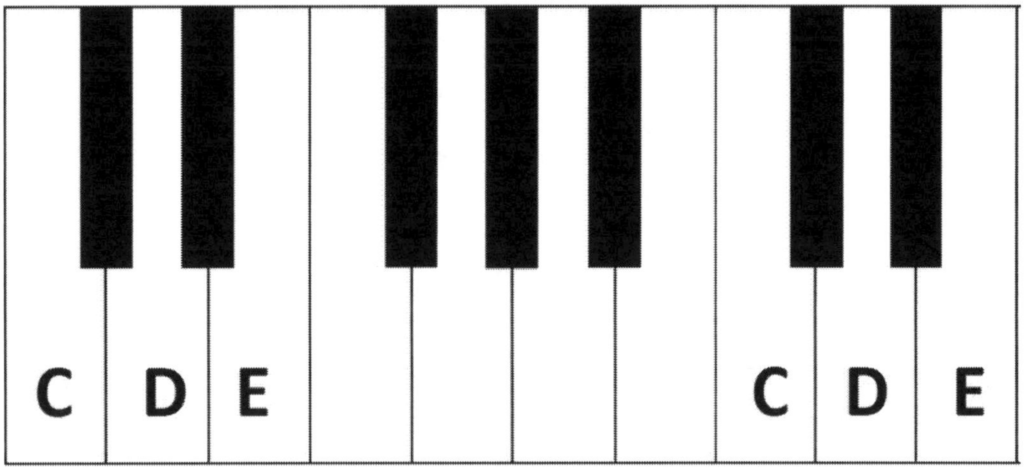
C D E
C D E

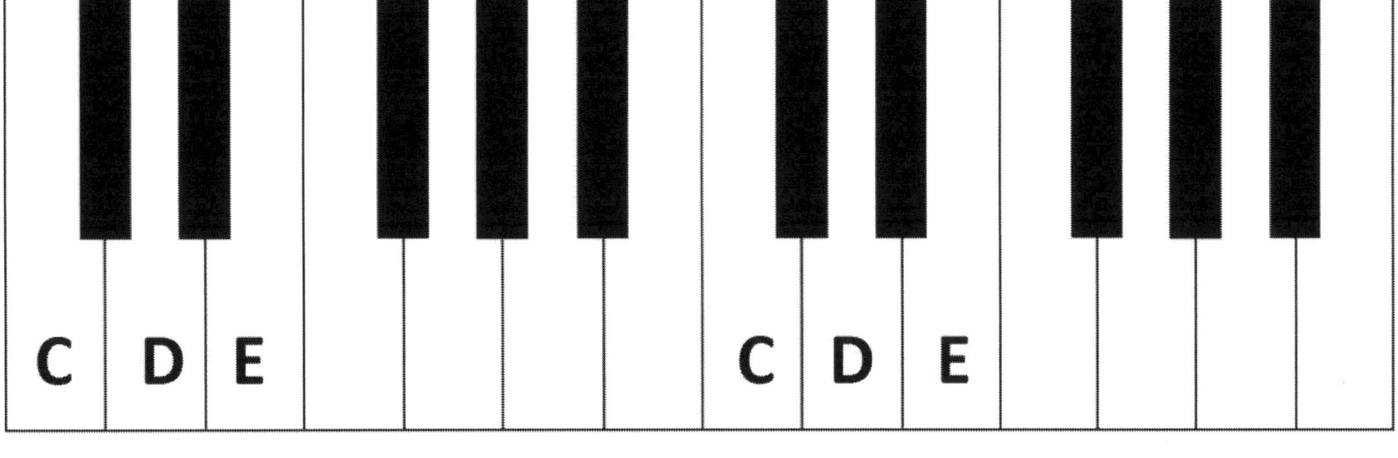
C D E
C D E

♩ = ♡   Quarter Note

𝅗𝅥 = ♡ ♡   Half Note

*in most songs

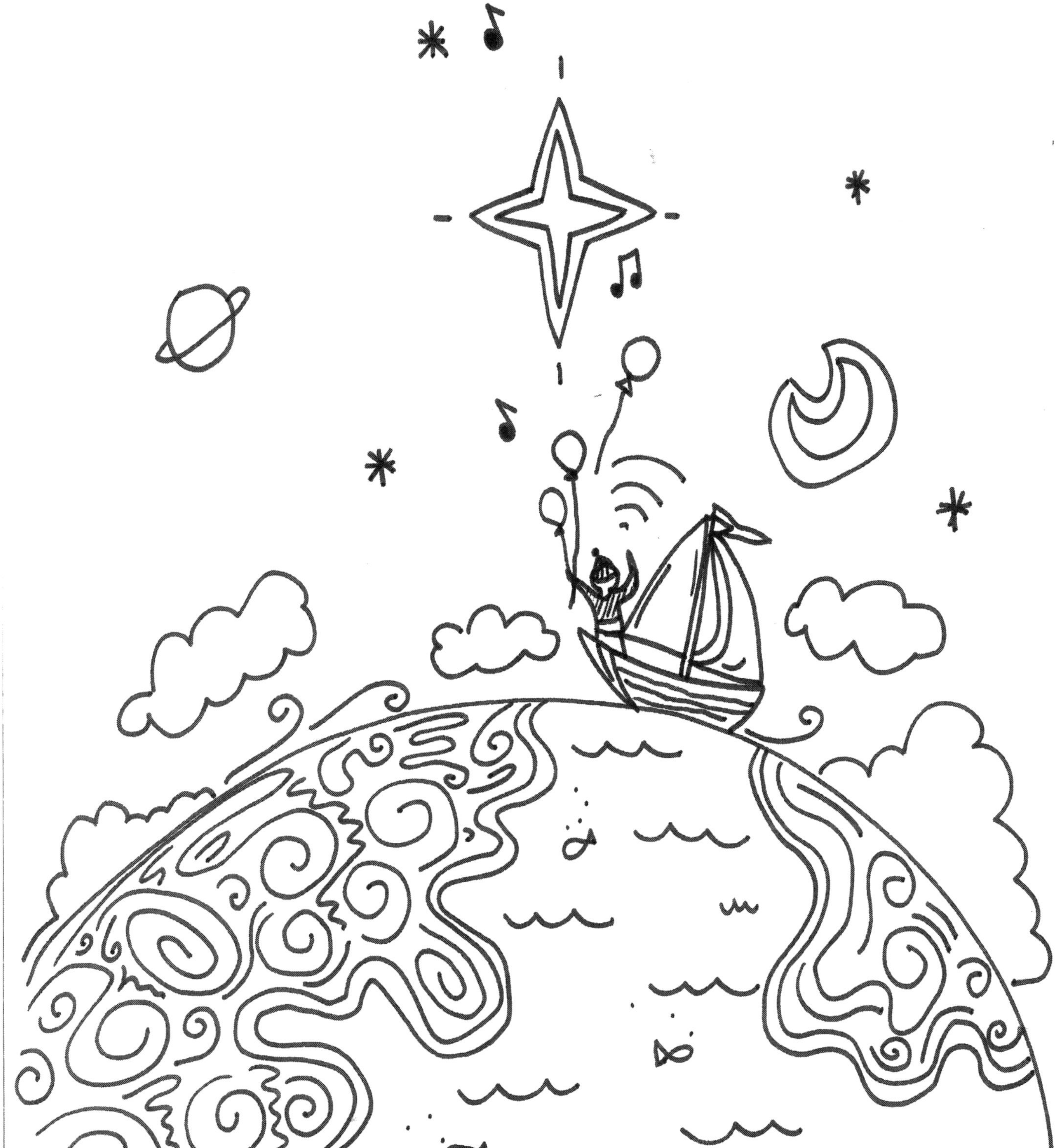

PICNIC

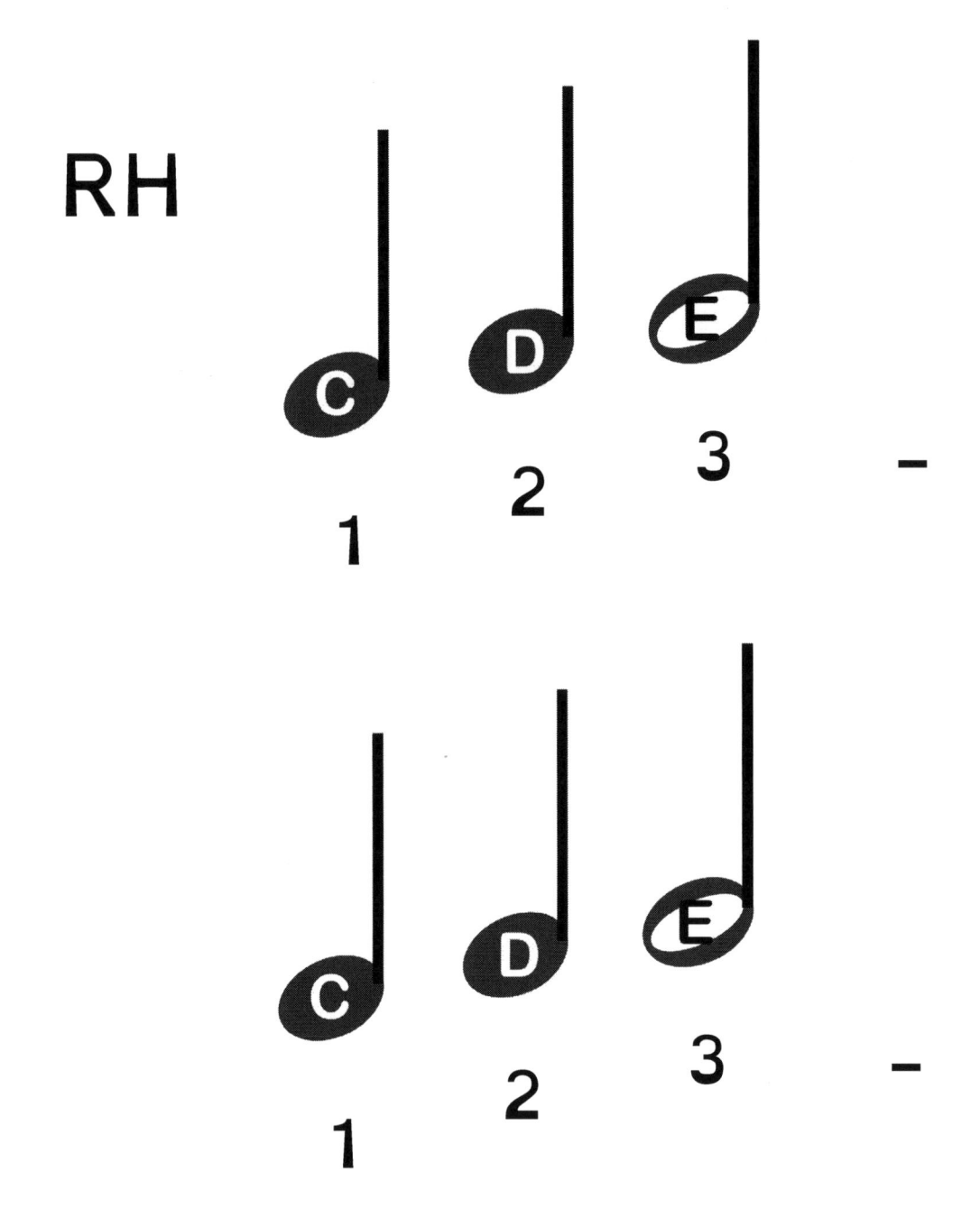

RH

C	D	E	—
1	2	3	—

C	D	E	—
1	2	3	—

E   D   C
3   2   1   -

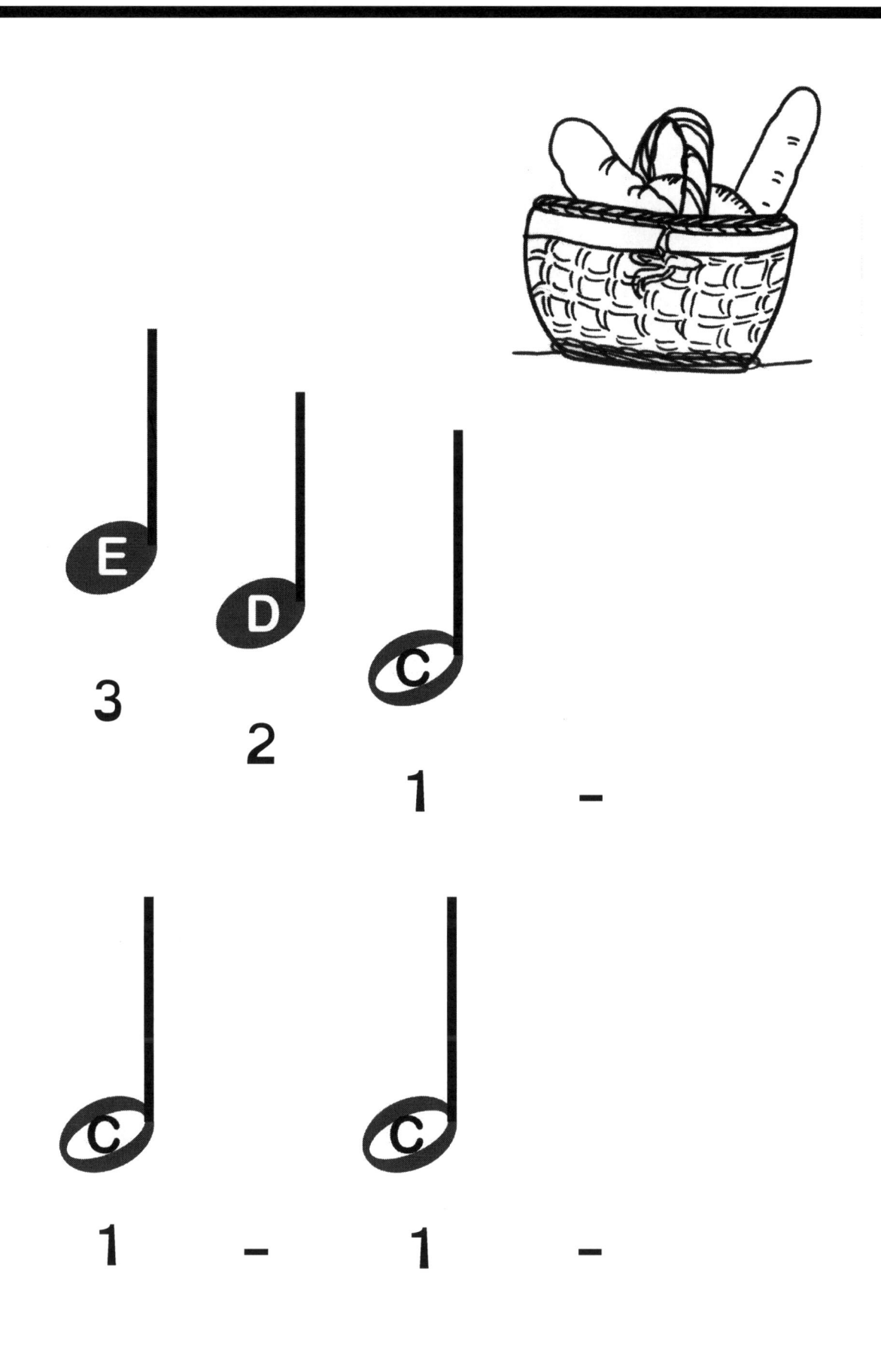

C   C
1   -   1   -

104

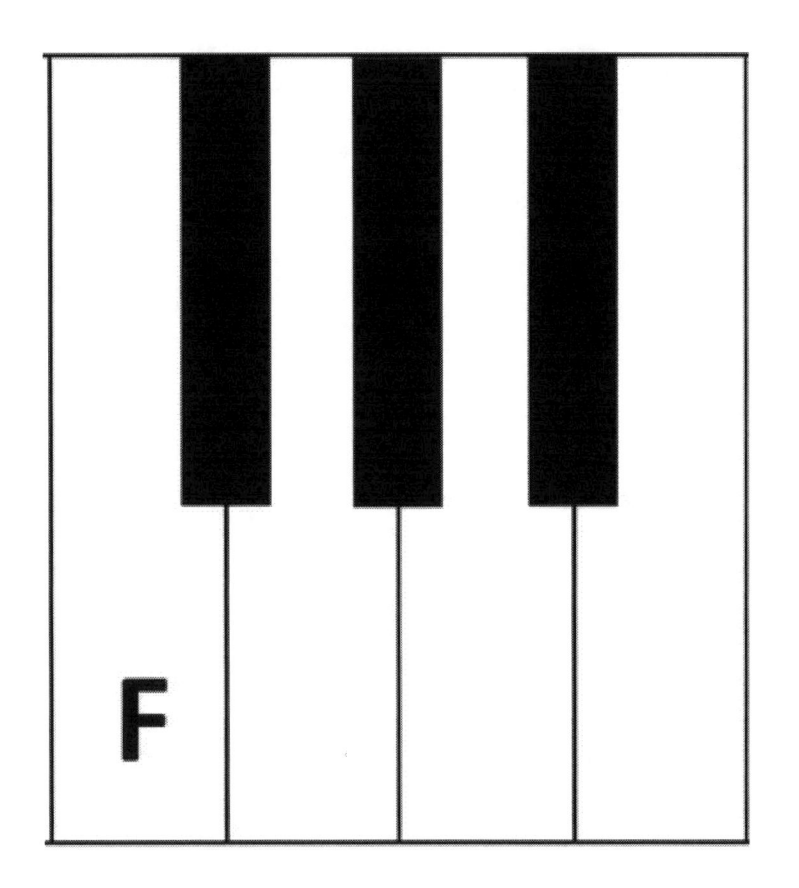

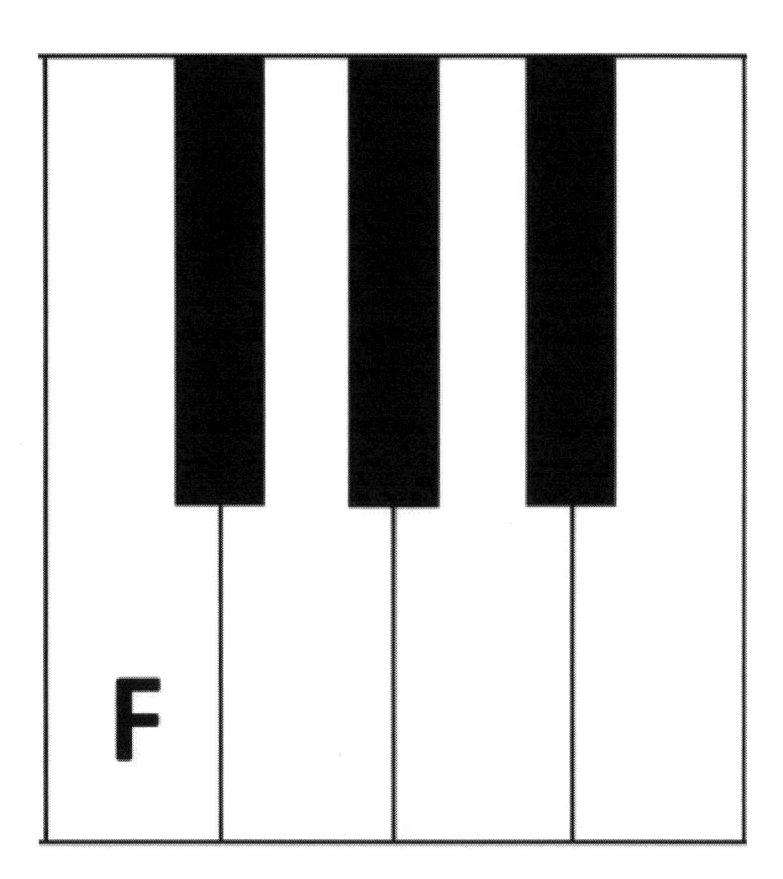

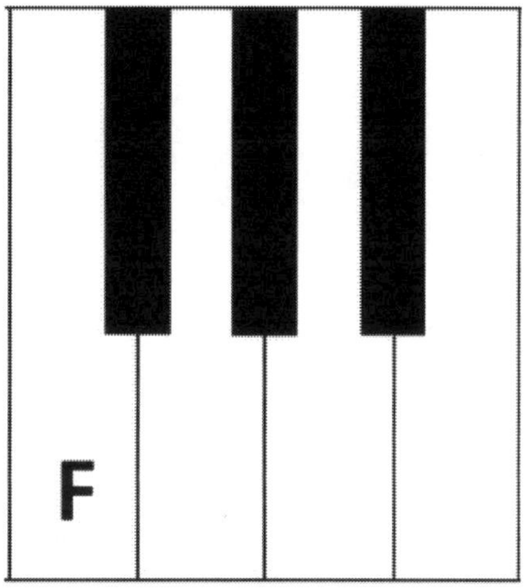
F

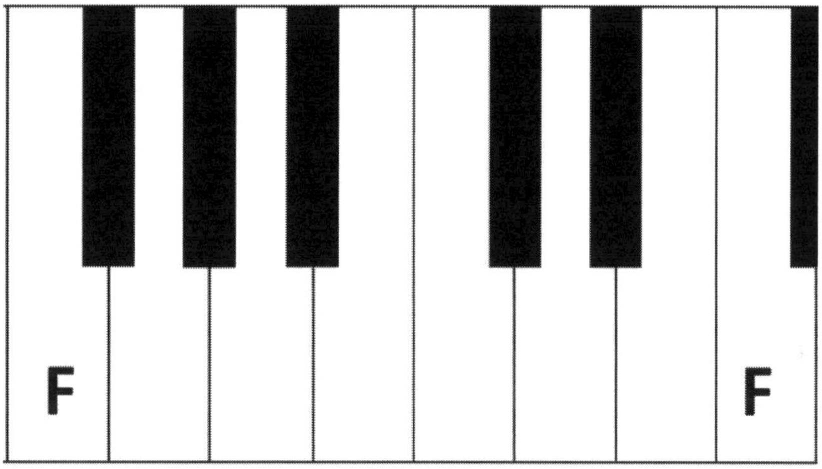
F
F

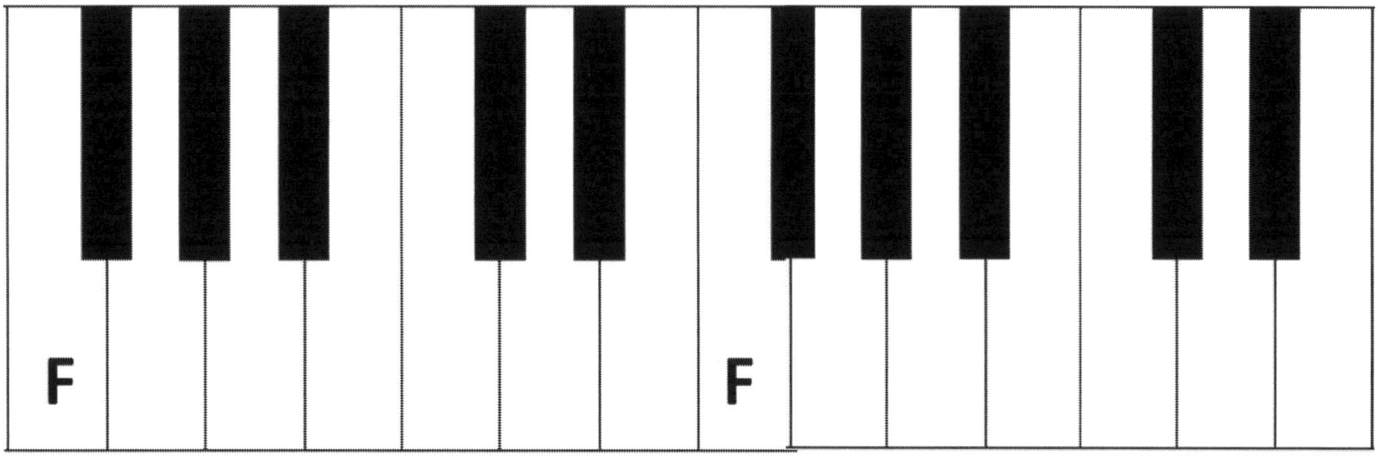
F
F

SWINGS

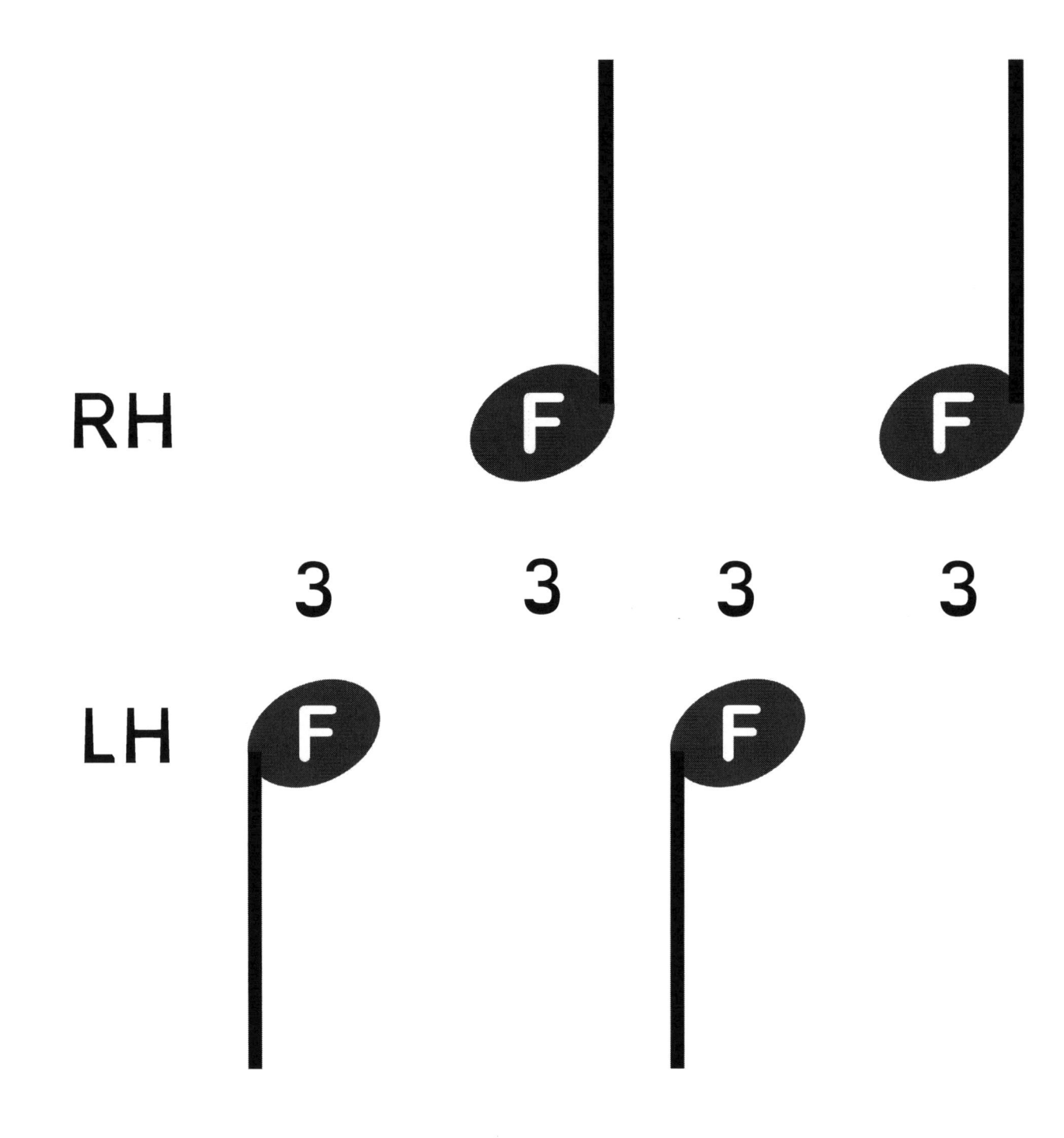

RH   F   F

   3   3   3   3

LH F   F

RH

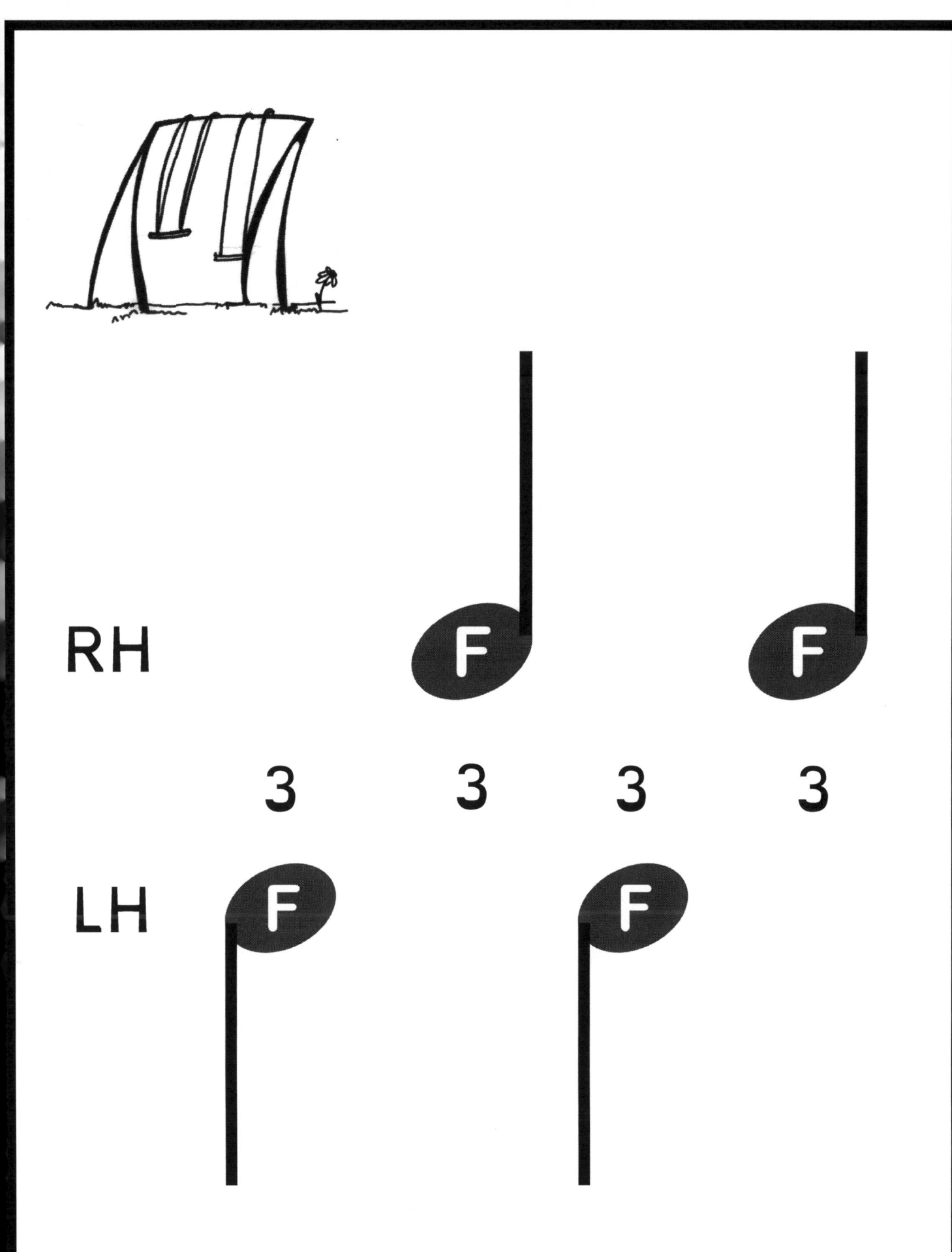

3 3 3 3

LH

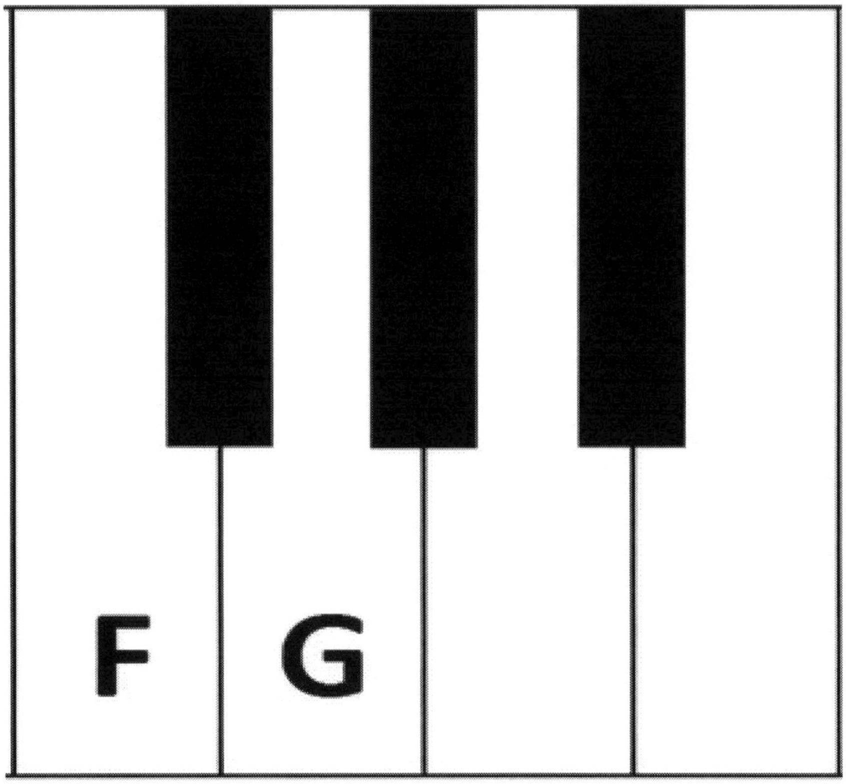
F
G

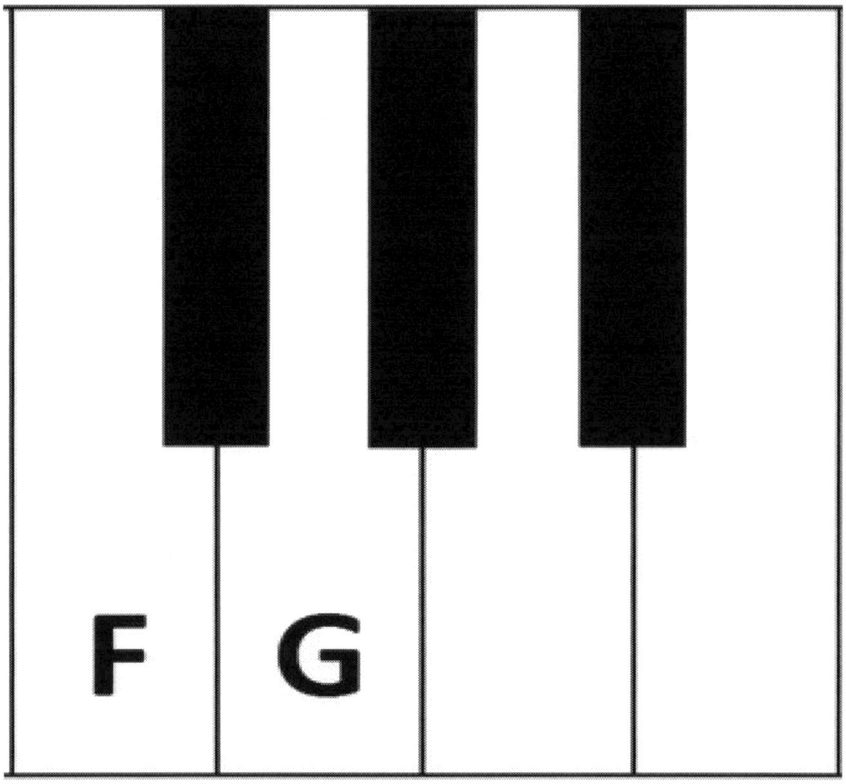
F
G

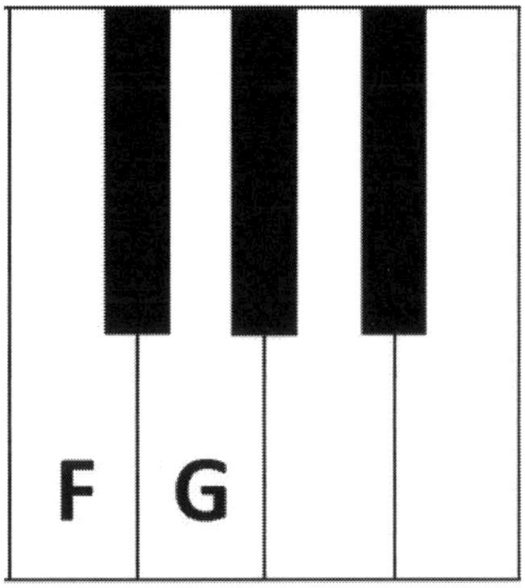
F
G

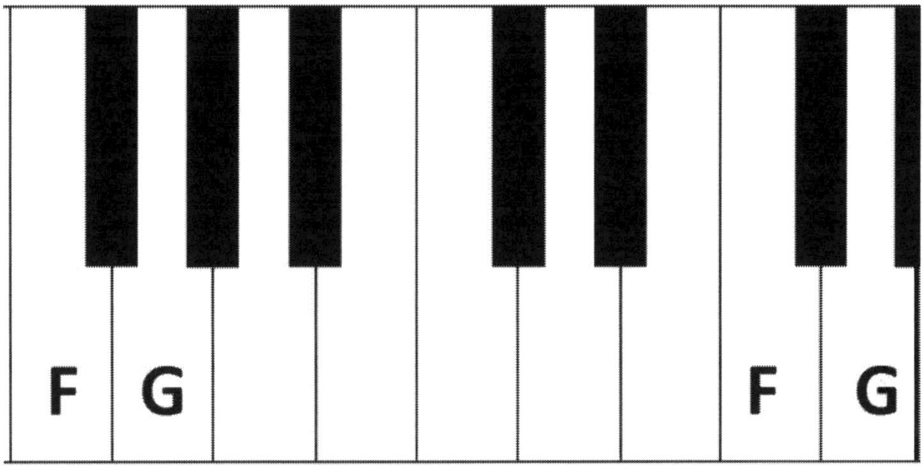
F
G
F
G

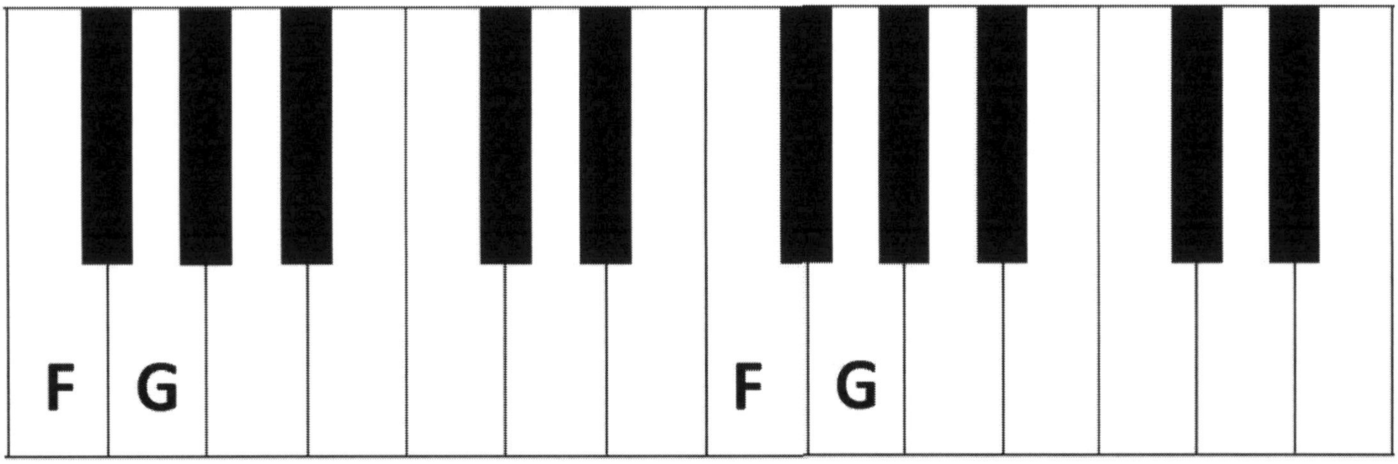
F
G
F
G

ALIENS

LH

3	3	3	3
F	F	F	F

2	2	2	2
G	G	G	G

3	-	2	-
F		G	

RH

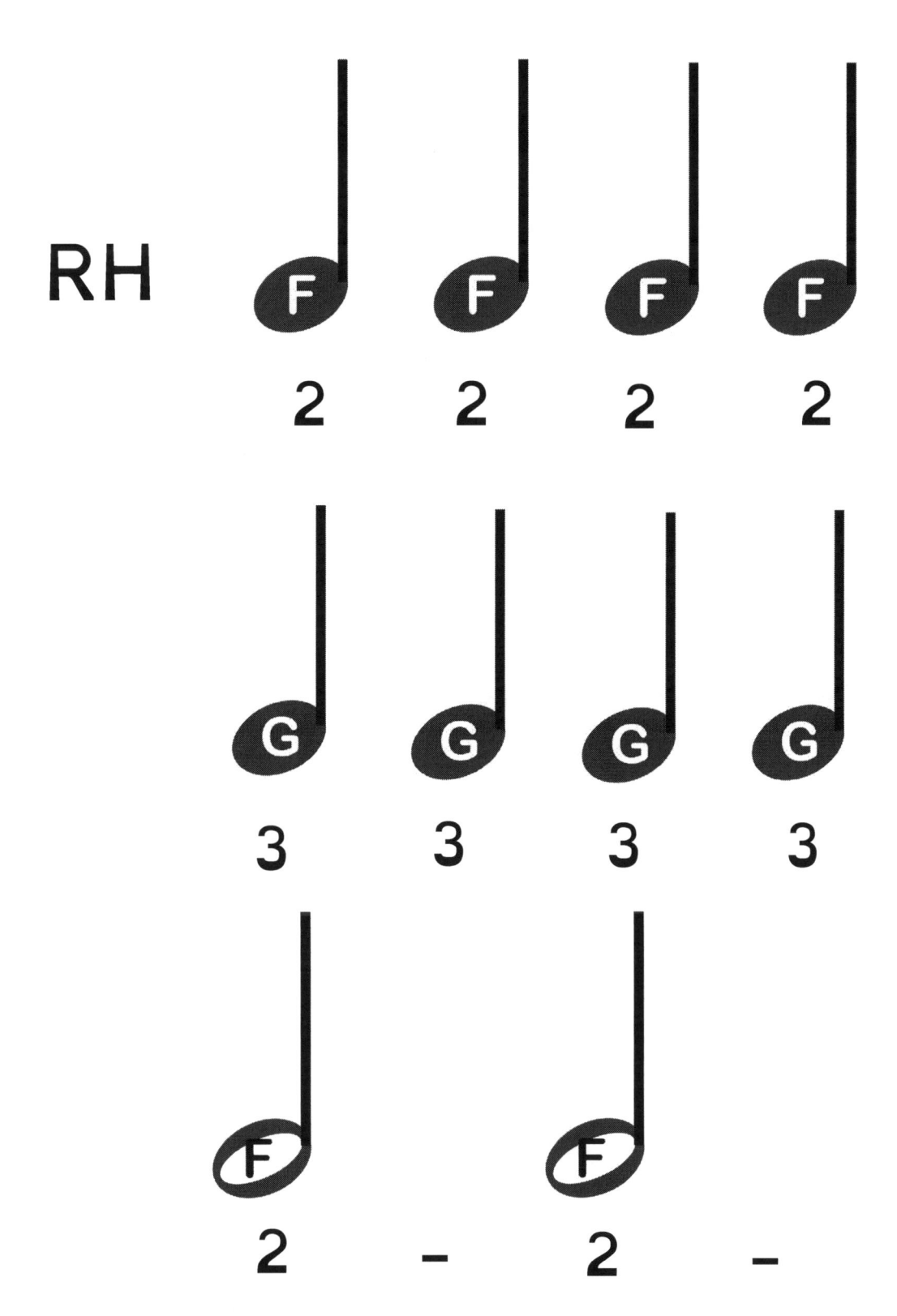

F F F F
2 2 2 2

G G G G
3 3 3 3

F   F
2 -   2 -

♩ = ♡   Quarter Note

𝅗𝅥 = ♡ ♡   Half Note

𝅗𝅥. = ♡ ♡ ♡   Dotted Half Note

𝅝 = ♡ ♡ ♡ ♡   Whole Note

*in most songs

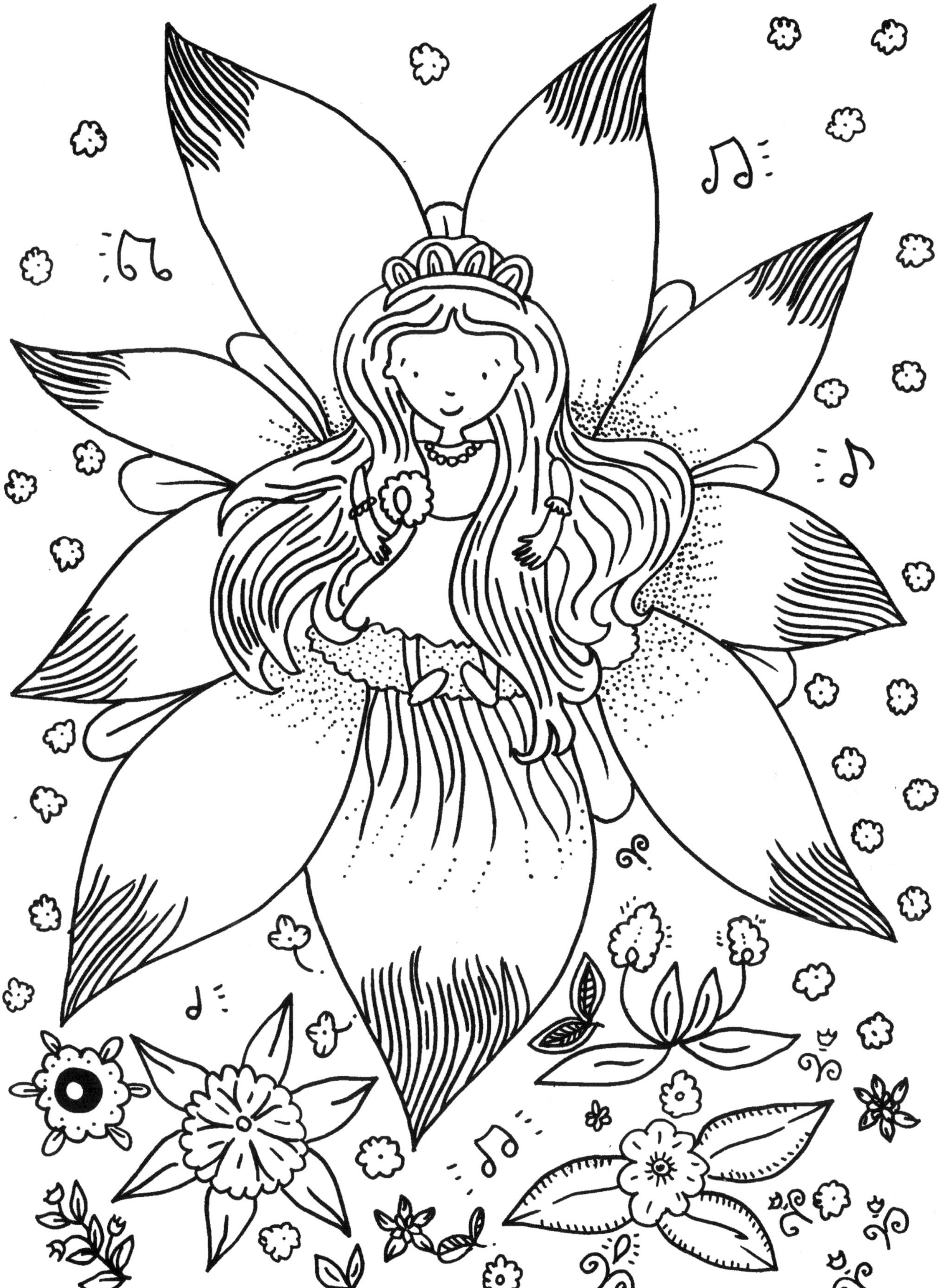

114

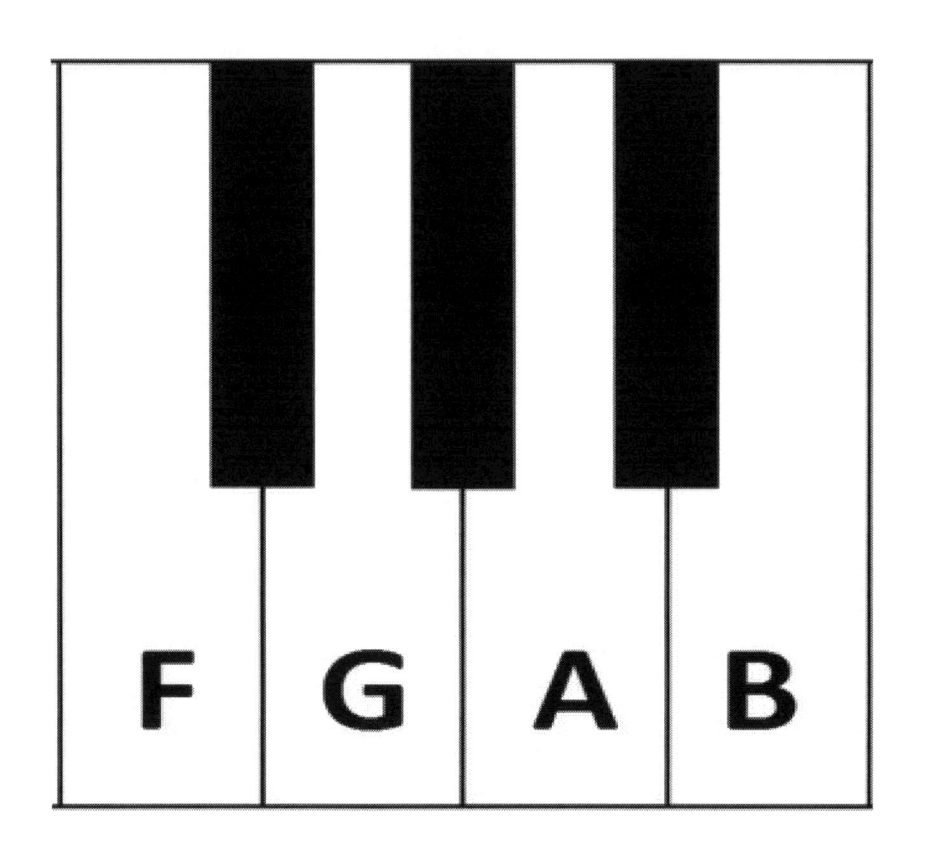

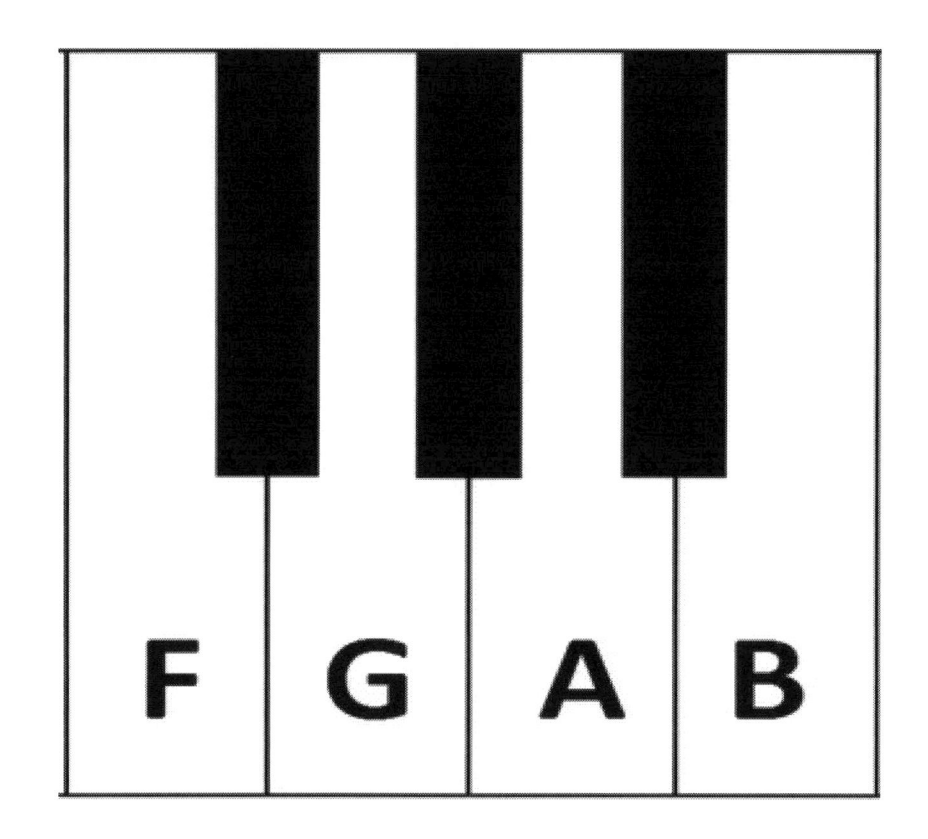

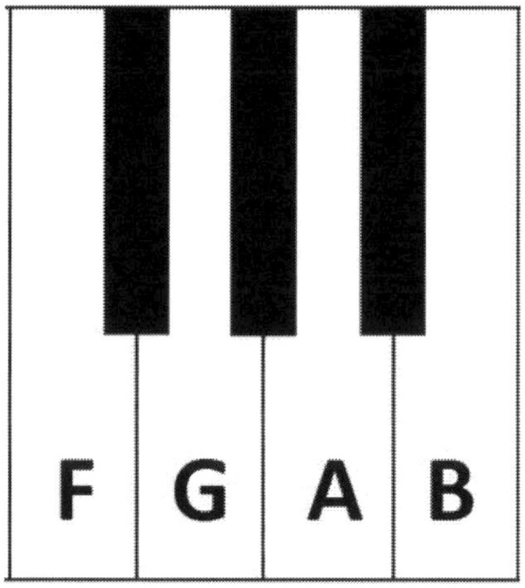
F G A B

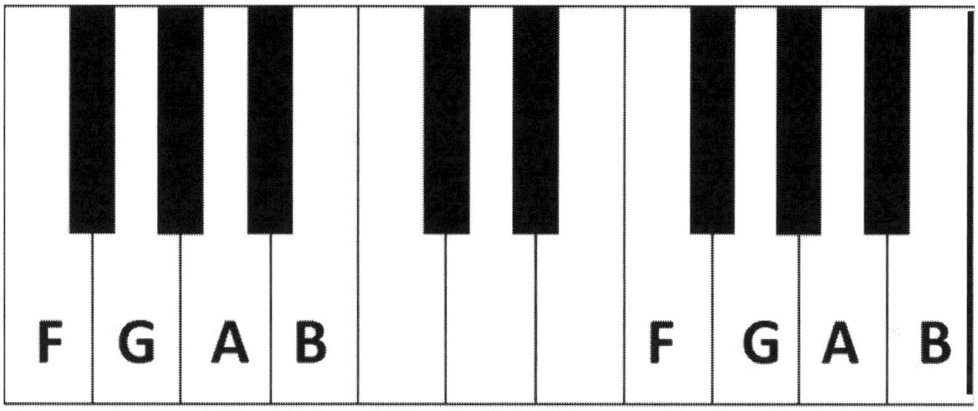
F G A B F G A B

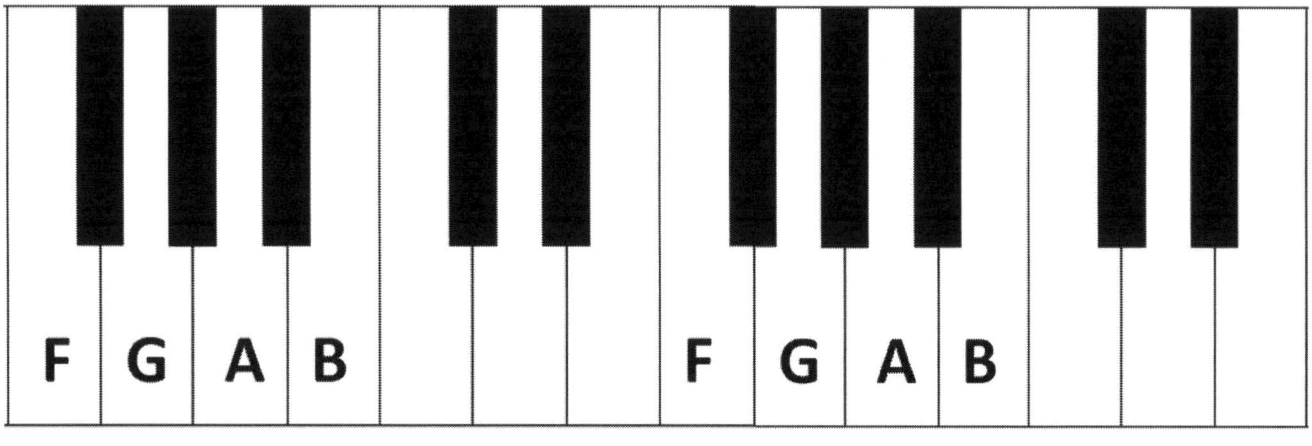
F G A B F G A B

OCEAN WAVES

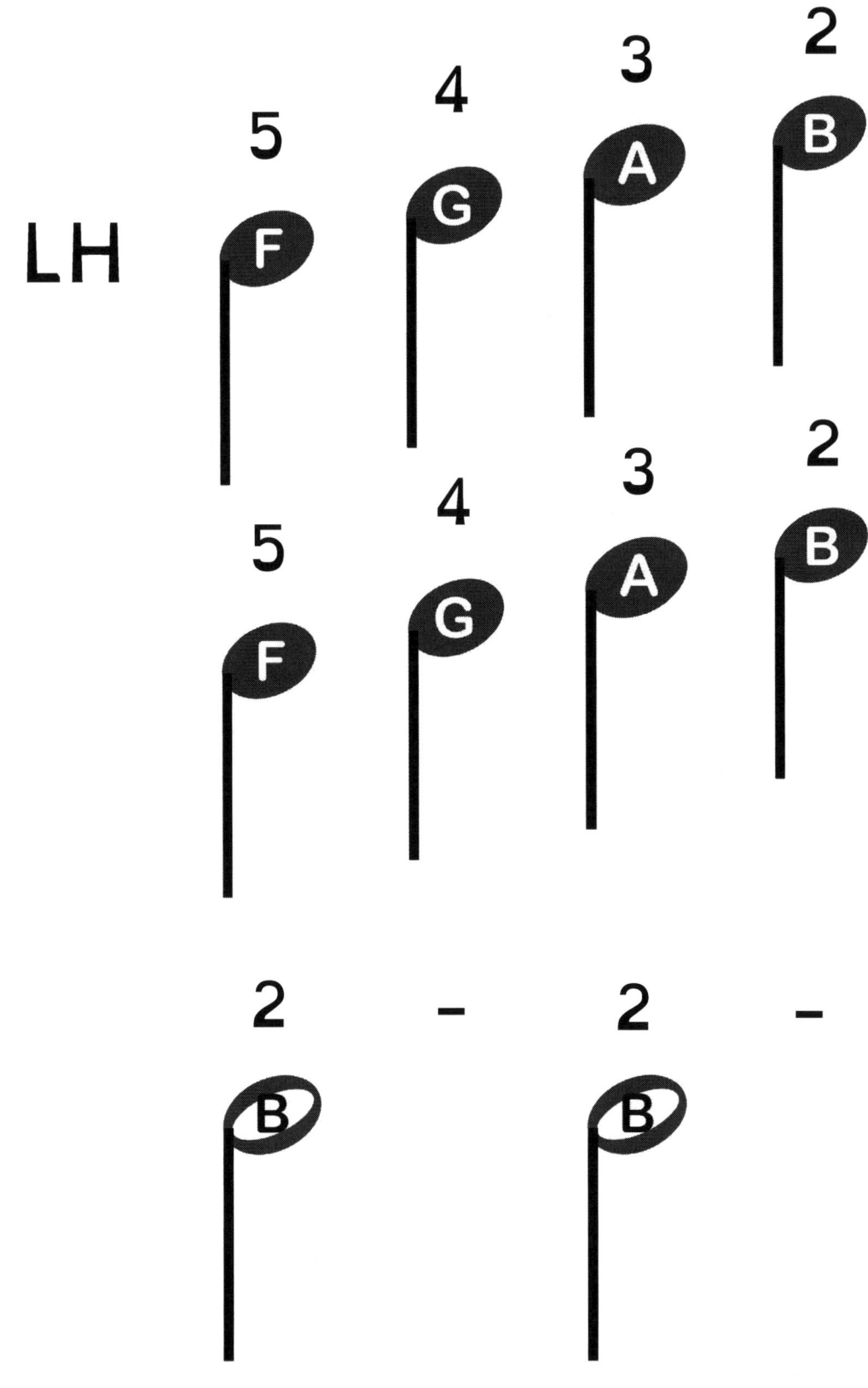

5	4	3	2
F	G	A	B

5	4	3	2
F	G	A	B

2	–	2	–
B		B	

LH

RH

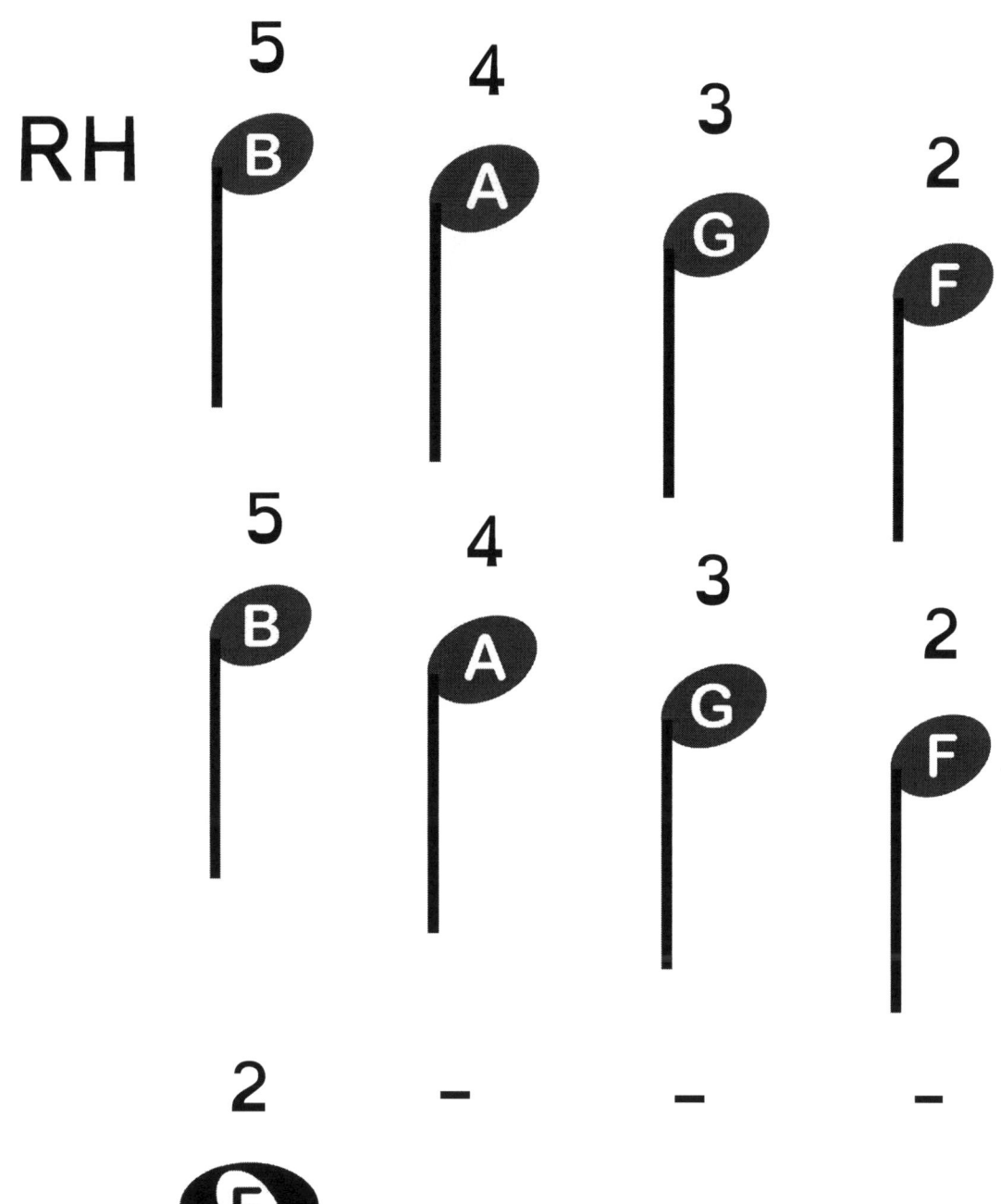

5	4	3	2
B	A	G	F

5	4	3	2
B	A	G	F

2 — — —
F

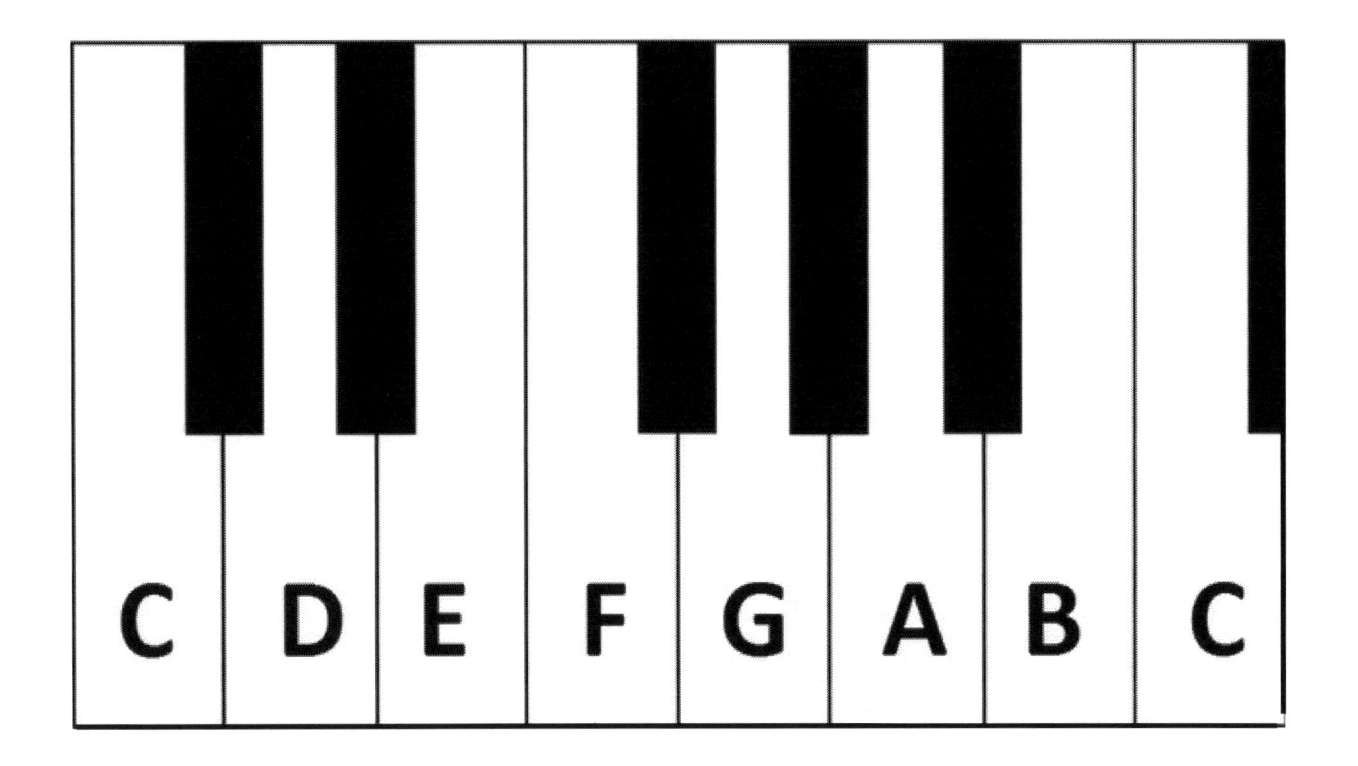

C SCALE = 8 notes

SCALE SCRAMBLE

Write the missing notes

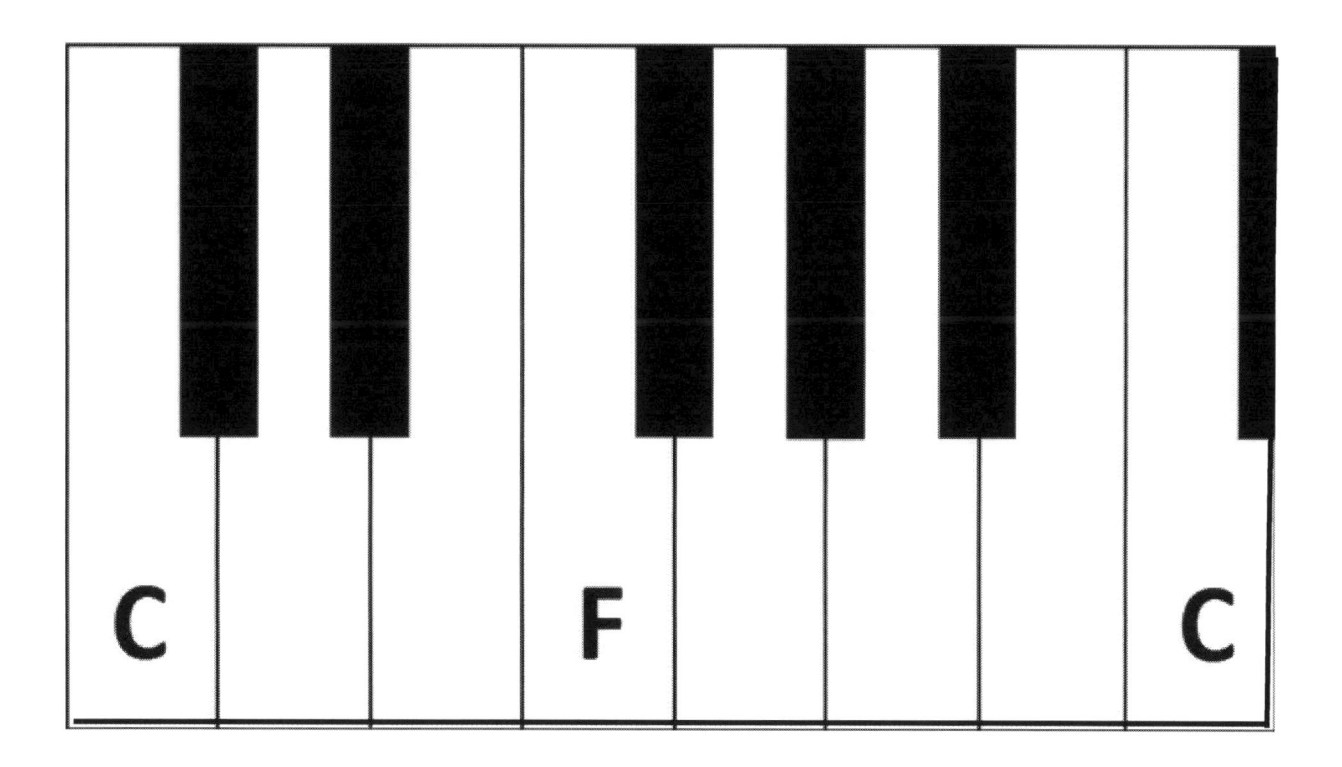

C   F   C

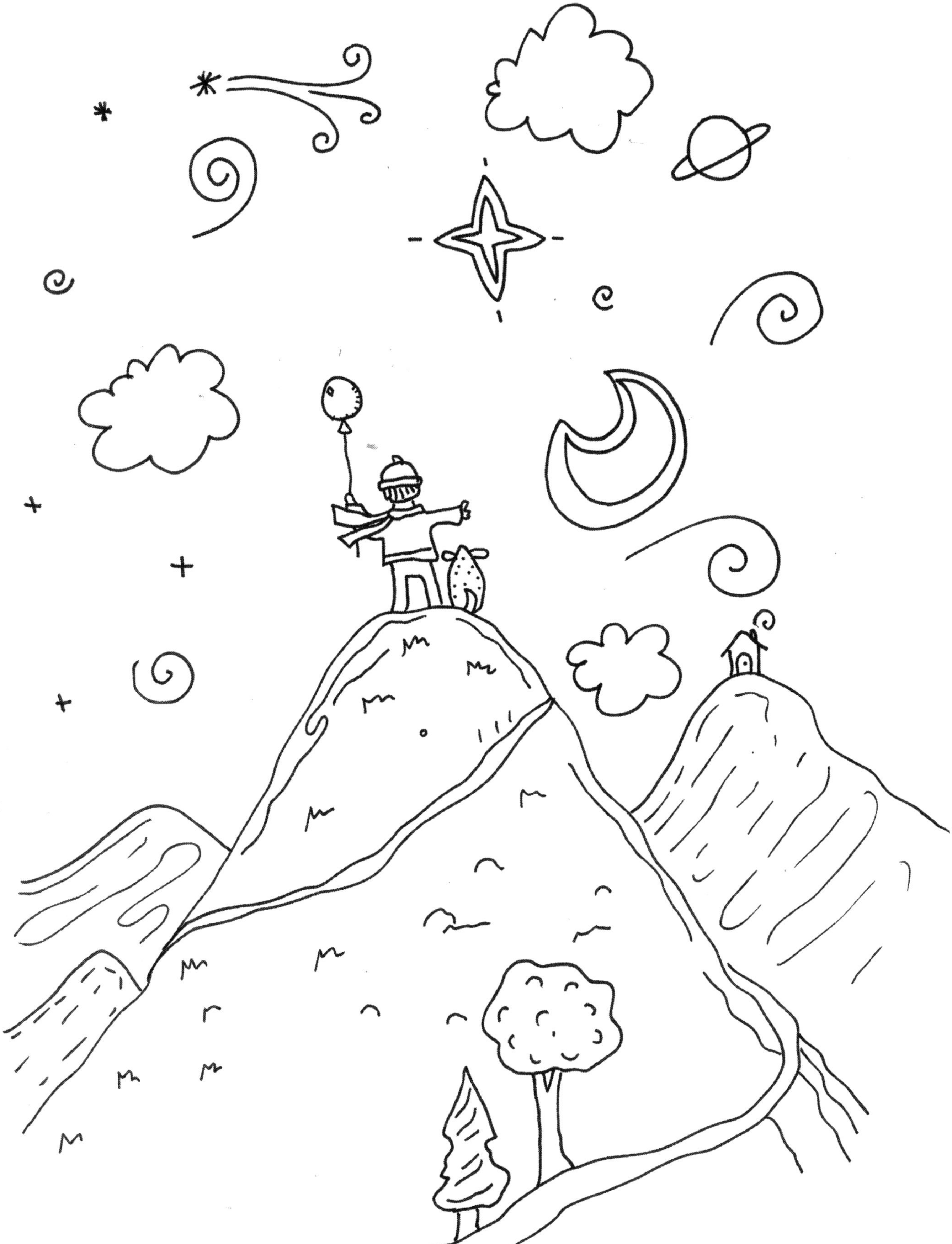

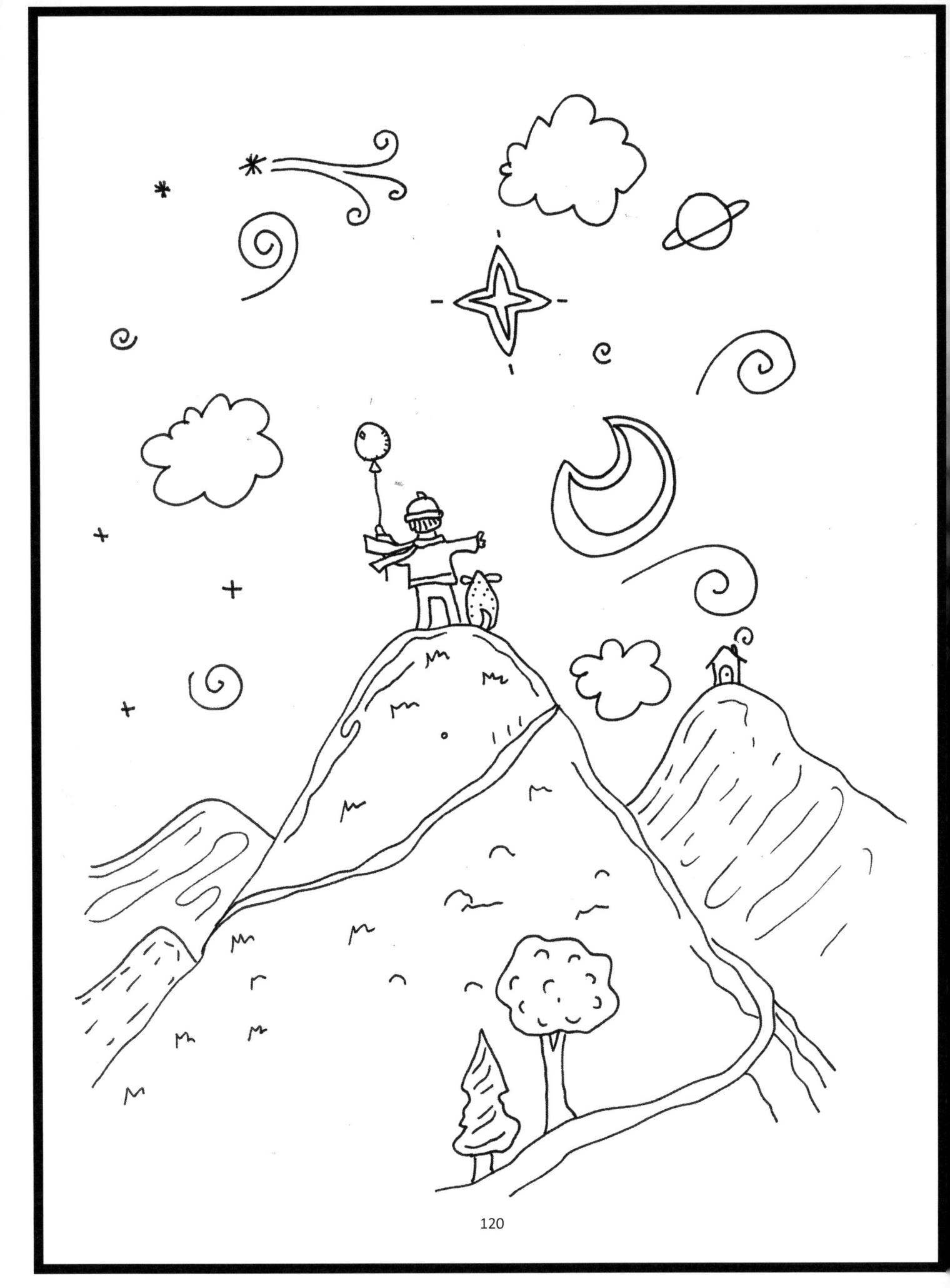

TWINKLE, TWINKLE, LITTLE STAR

Twinkle, twinkle, little star,
How I wonder what you are!
Up above the world so high,
Like a diamond in the sky.

Twinkle, twinkle, little star,
How I wonder what you are!

C C G G A A G F F E E D D C

G G F F E E D G G F F E E D

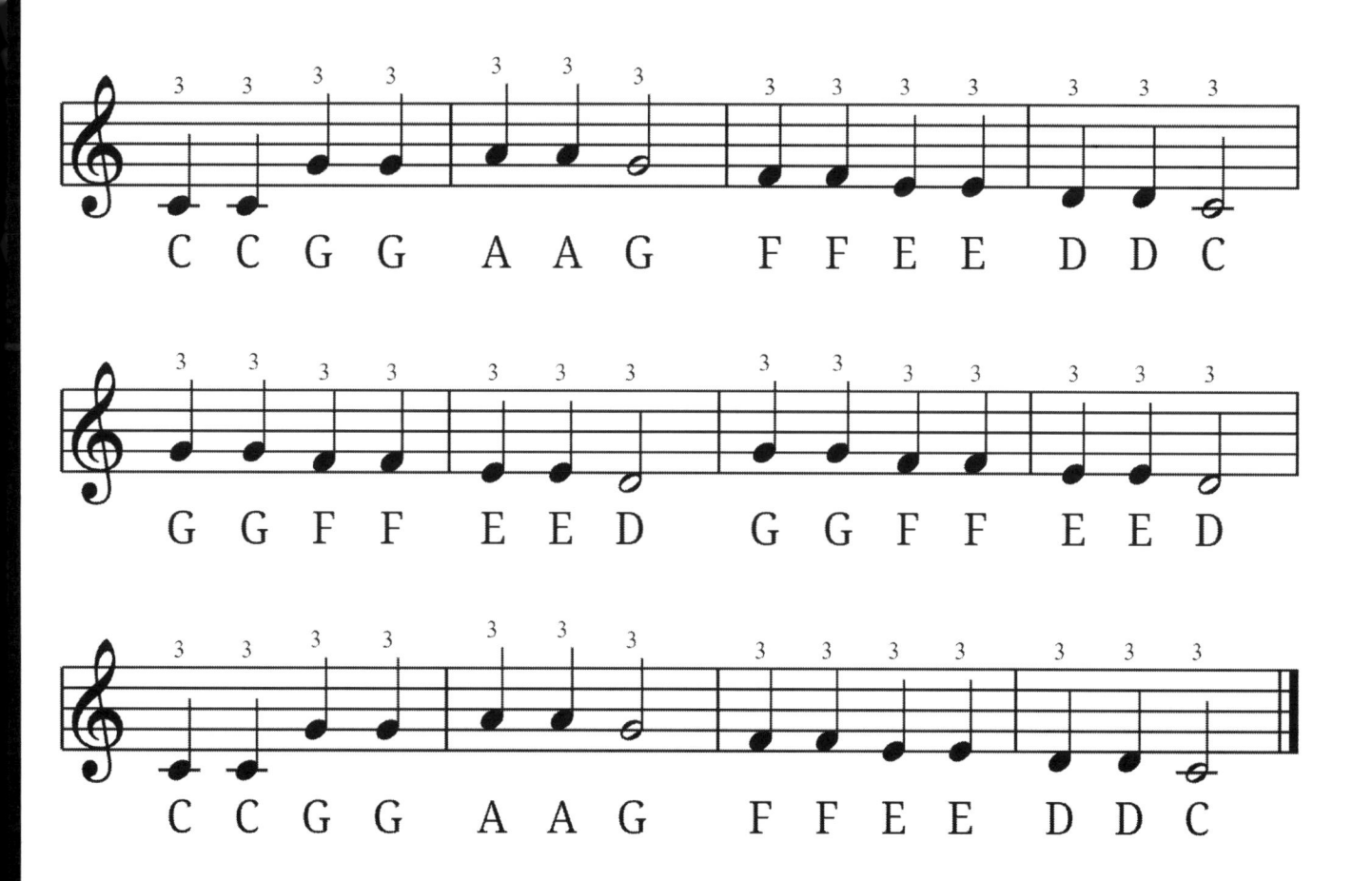

C C G G A A G F F E E D D C

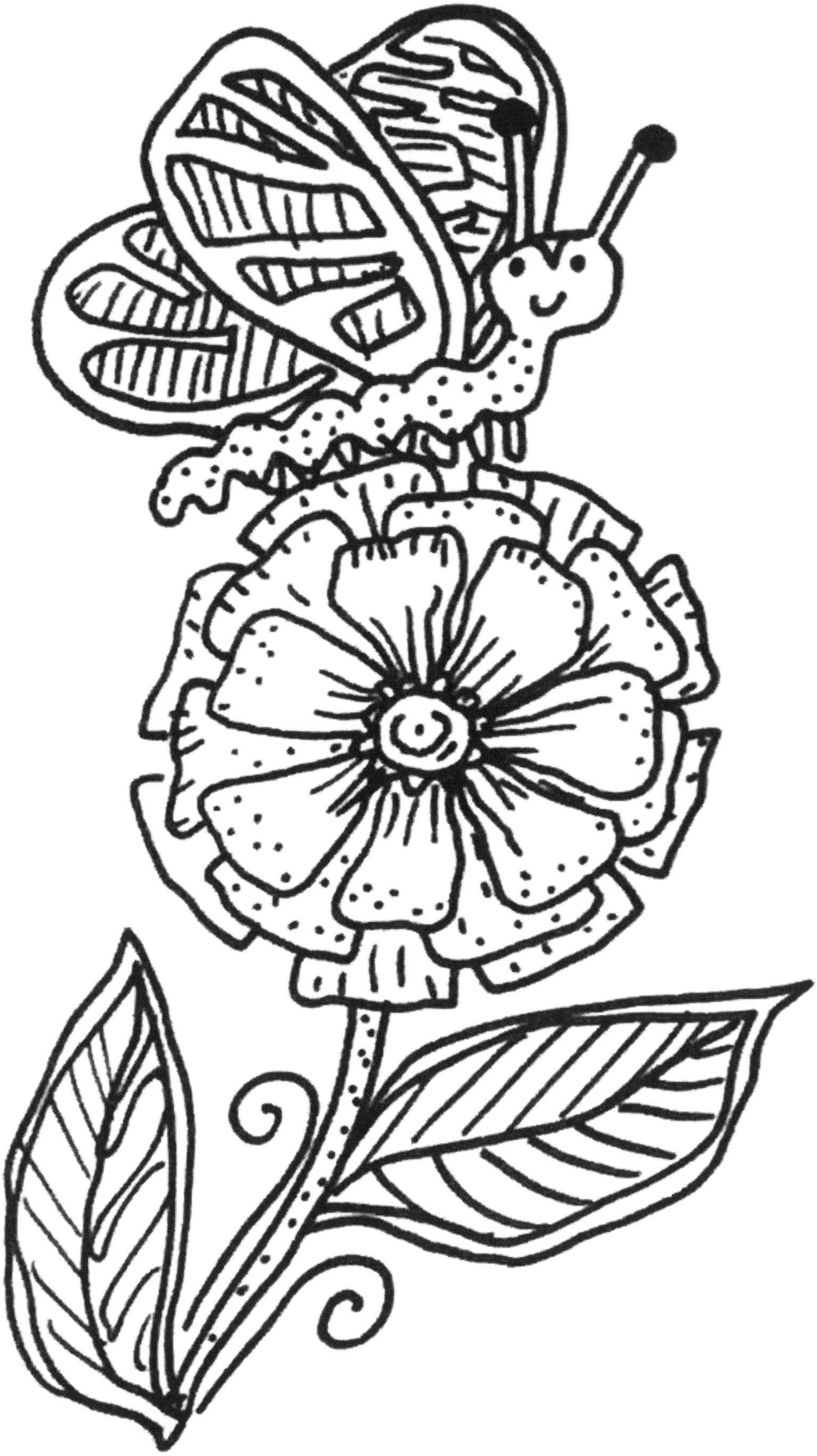

ODE TO JOY

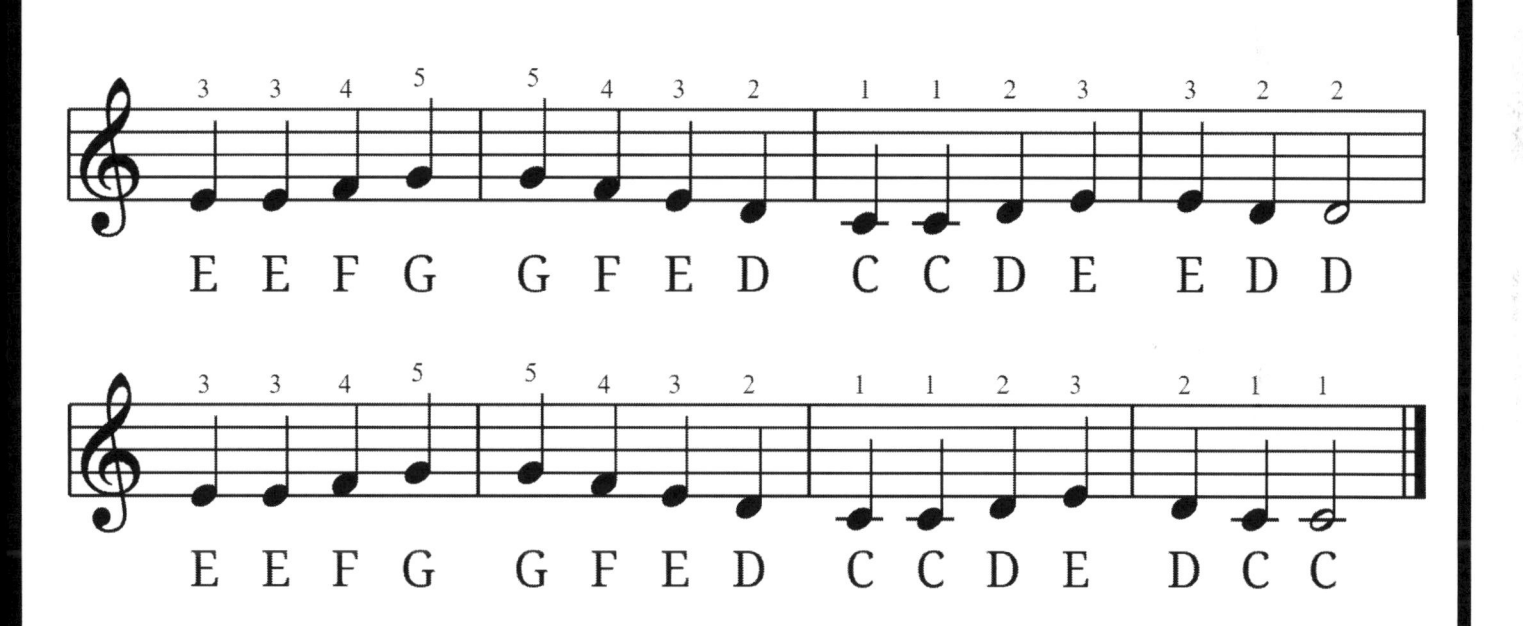

E E F G G F E D C C D E E D D

E E F G G F E D C C D E D C C

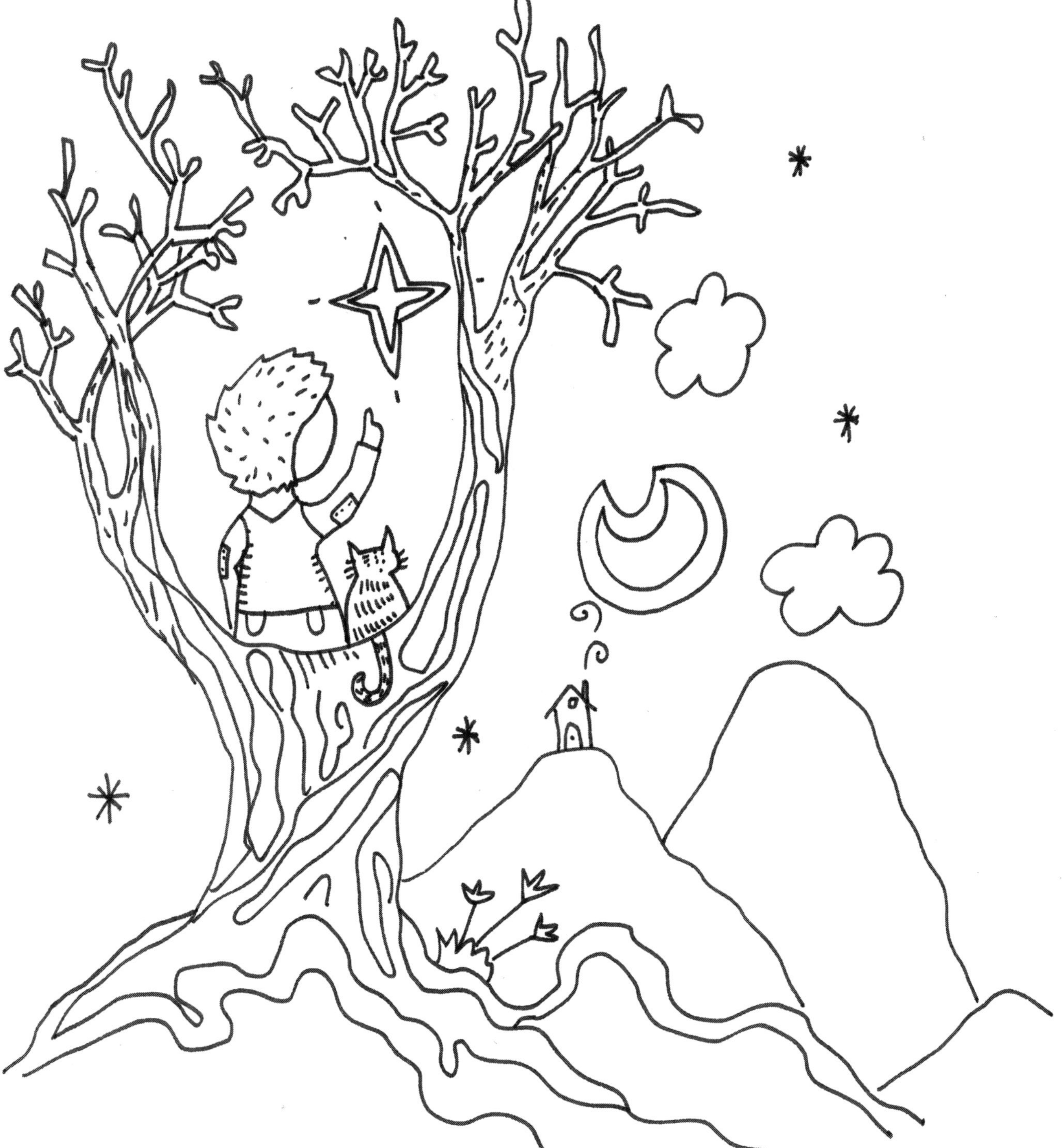

STAR LIGHT, STAR BRIGHT

Star light, star bright,

The first star I see tonight;

I wish I may, I wish I might,

Have the wish I wish tonight.

— Anonymous

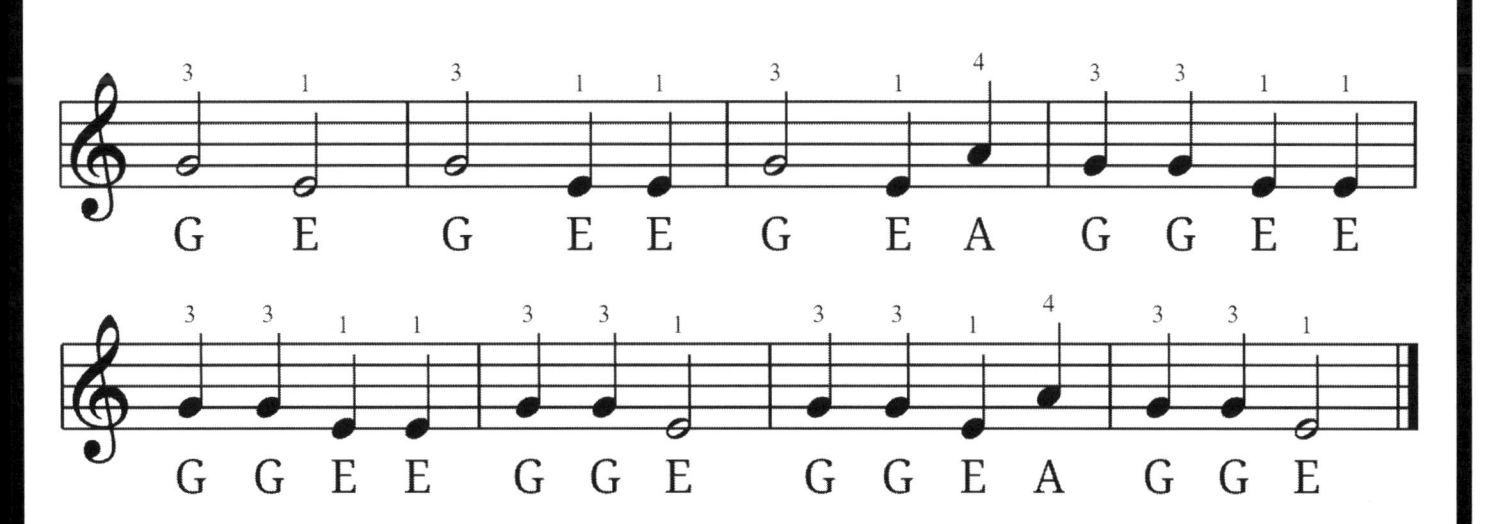

JINGLE BELLS

Jingle bells,

Jingle bells

Jingle all the way

Oh, what fun it is to ride

In a one horse open sleigh, hey!

Jingle bells, jingle bells

Jingle all the way

Oh, what fun it is to ride

In a one horse open sleigh!

— Pierpont

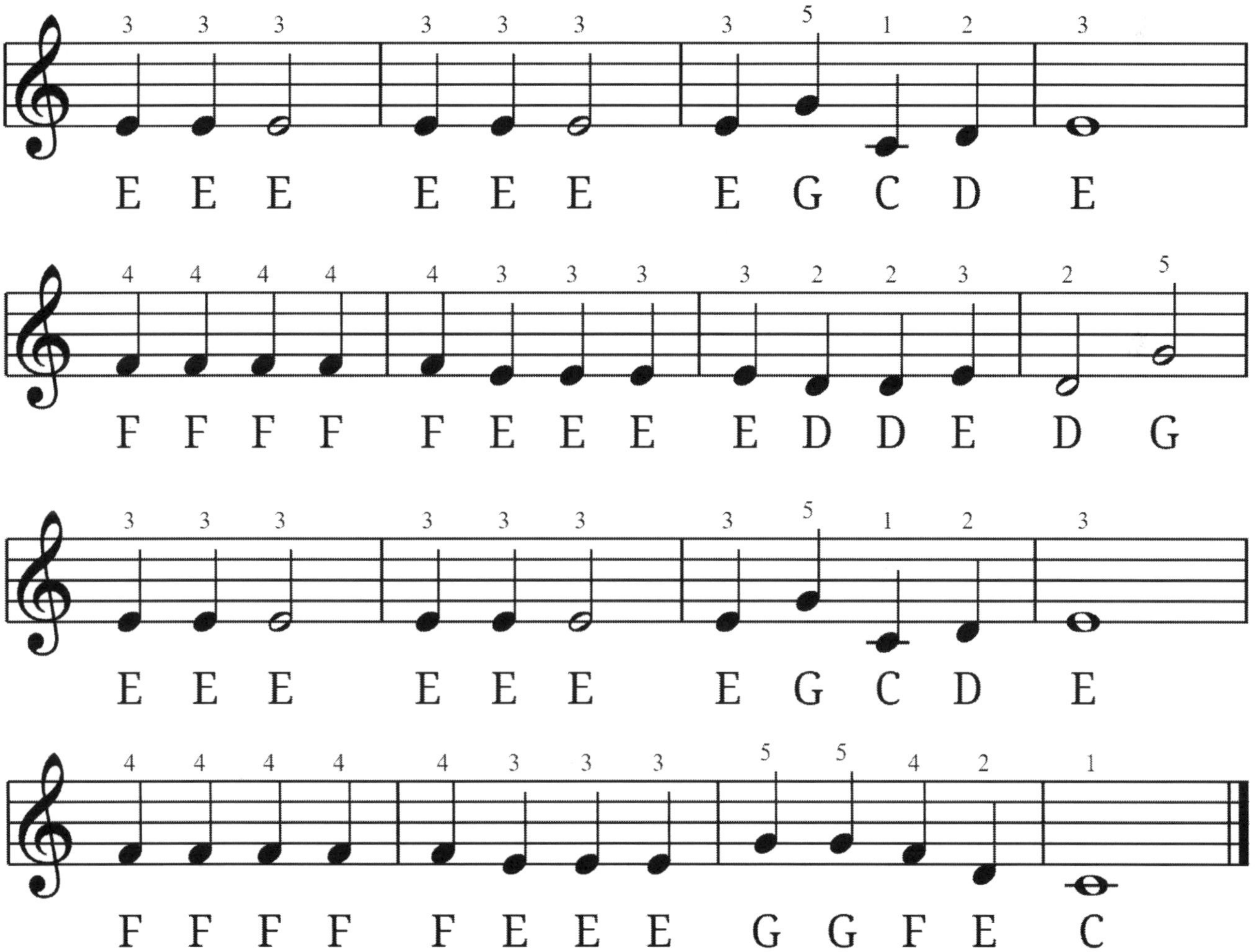
3 3 3 3 3 3 3 5 1 2 3
E E E E E E E G C D E
4 4 4 4 4 3 3 3 3 2 2 3 2 5
F F F F F E E E E D D E D G
3 3 3 3 3 3 3 5 1 2 3
E E E E E E E G C D E
4 4 4 4 4 3 3 3 5 5 4 2 1
F F F F F E E E G G F E C

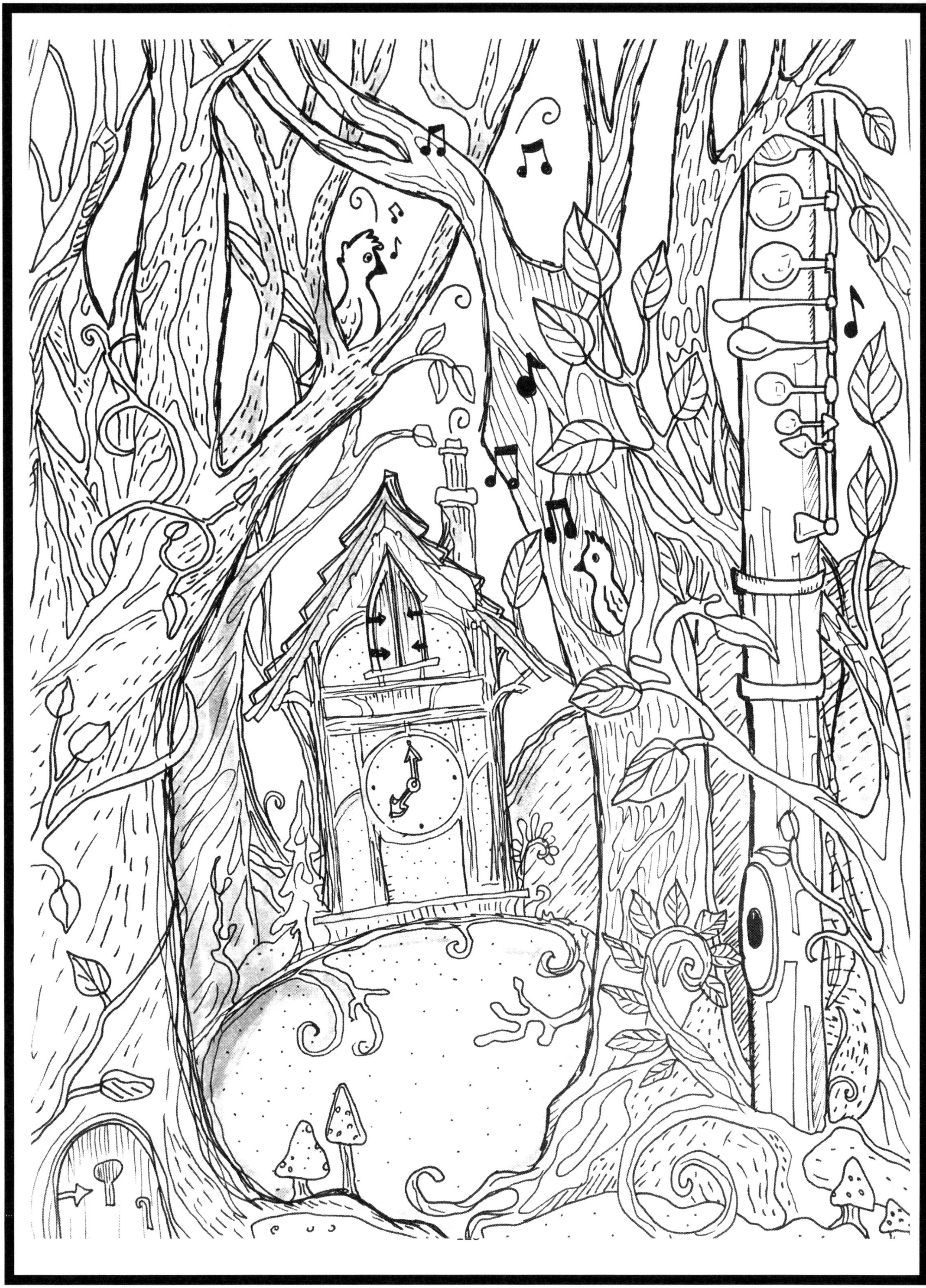

WESTMINSTER CHIMES

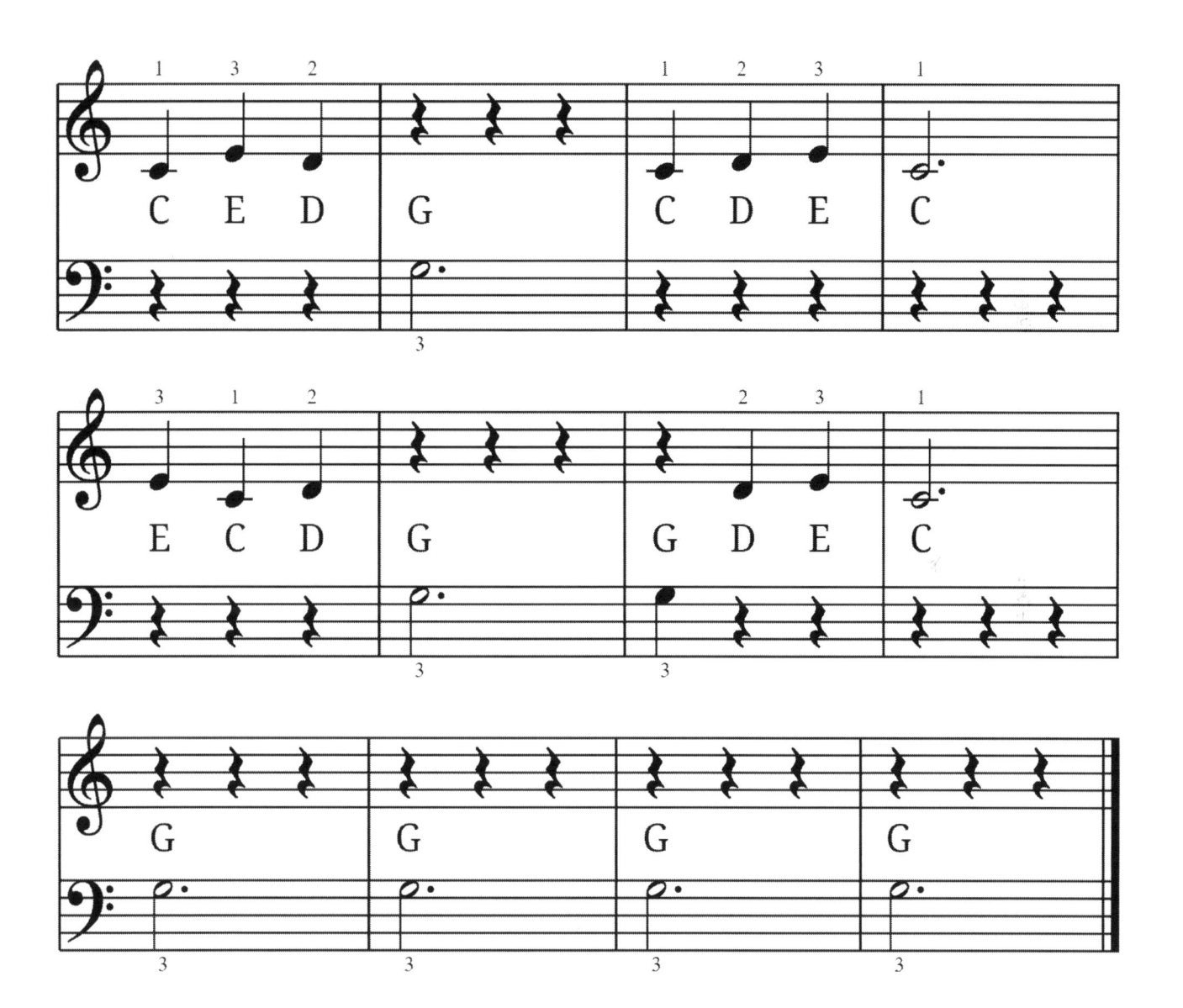

OLD MACDONALD

Old MacDonald had a farm,

E-I-E-I-O.

And on his farm he had some chicks,

E-I-E-I-O.

With a chick, chick here,

And a chick, chick there,

Here a chick, there a chick,

Everywhere a chick, chick,

Old MacDonald had a farm,

E-I-E-I-O.

131

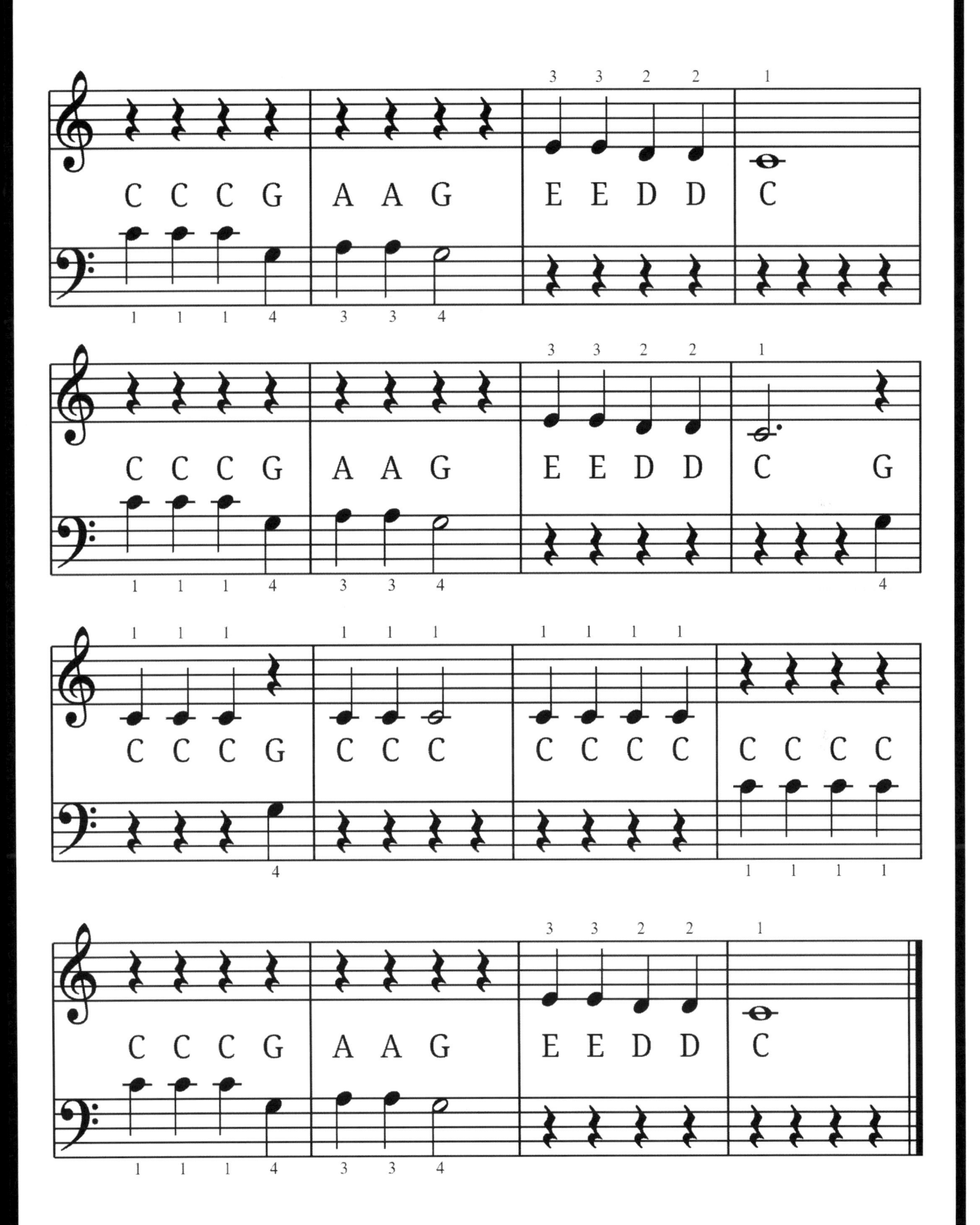

OLD MACDONALD
(continued)

2. Duck - quack

3. Turkey - gobble

4. Pig - oink, oink

5. Cow - moo, moo

6. Cat - meow, meow

7. Mule - Heehaw

8. Dog - bow wow

- Traditional

133

JOLLY OLD ST. NICHOLAS

Jolly old St. Nicholas
Lean your ear this way
Don't you tell a single soul
What I'm going to say

Christmas Eve is coming soon
Now, you dear old man
Whisper what you'll bring to me
Tell me if you can

— Miller & McCaskey

3 3 3 3 2 2 2 1 1 1 1 3
E E E E D D D C C C C E
2 1 2 3 2
A A A A G G C D C D E D
3 3 3 3 4 4 1
3 3 3 3 2 2 2 1 1 1 1 3
E E E E D D D C C C C E
2 1 2 3 1
A A A A G G C D C C E C
3 3 3 3 4 4 1

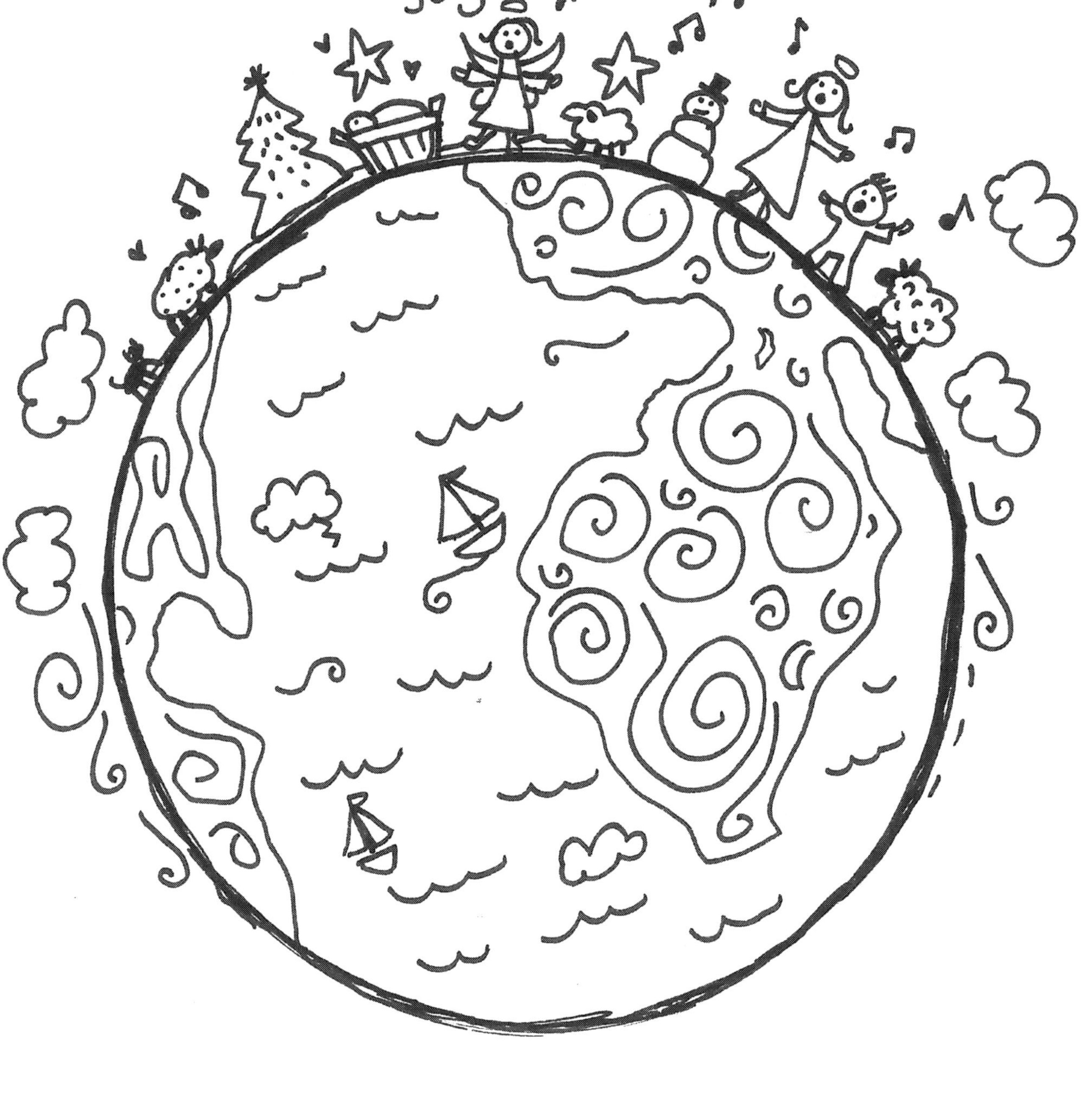
Joy!
Joy!

SUPER HERO

Make your own song

Start with "3" fingers

LEFT hand C's

RIGHT hand G's

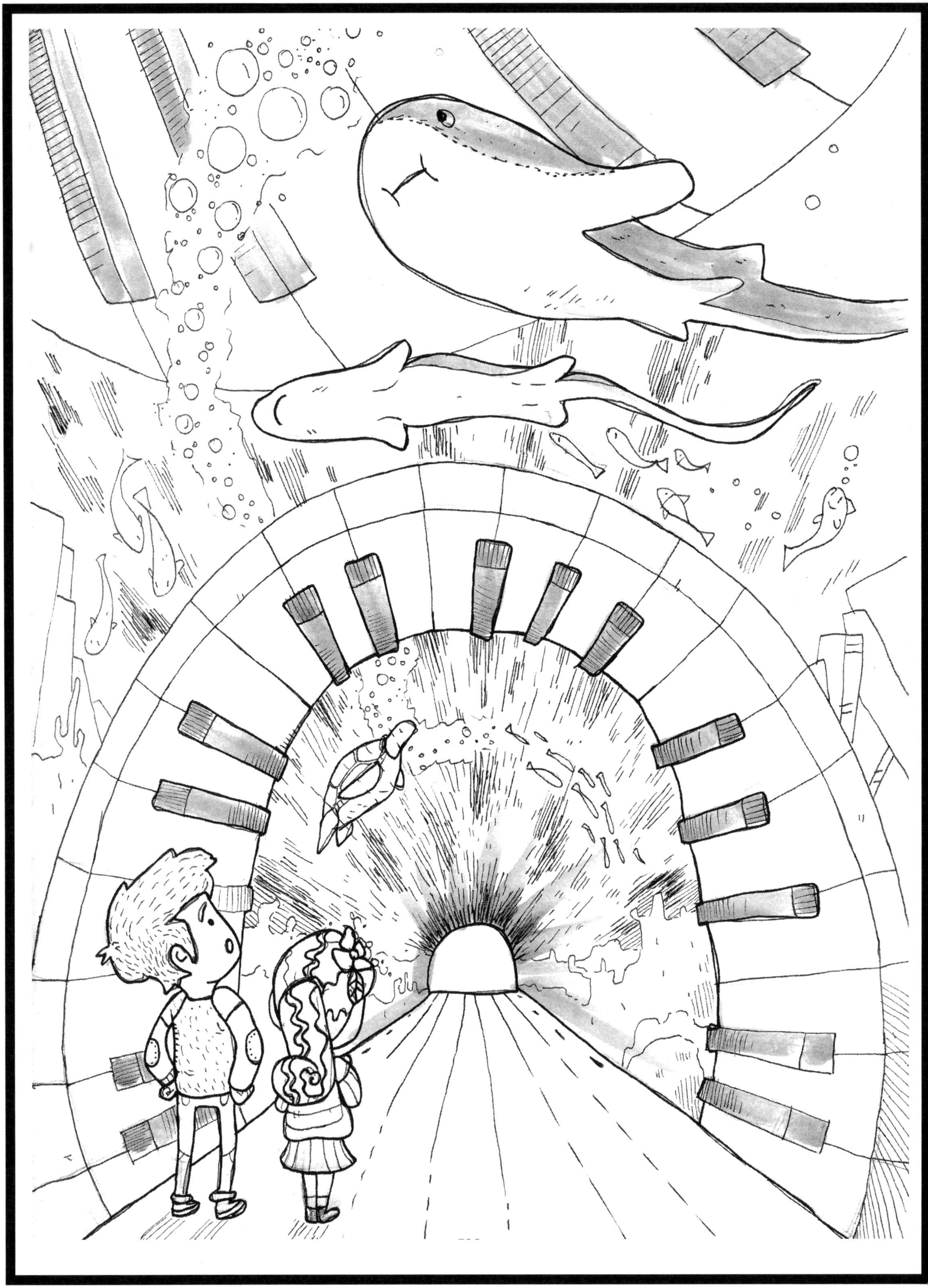

MOVE with the AQUARIUM

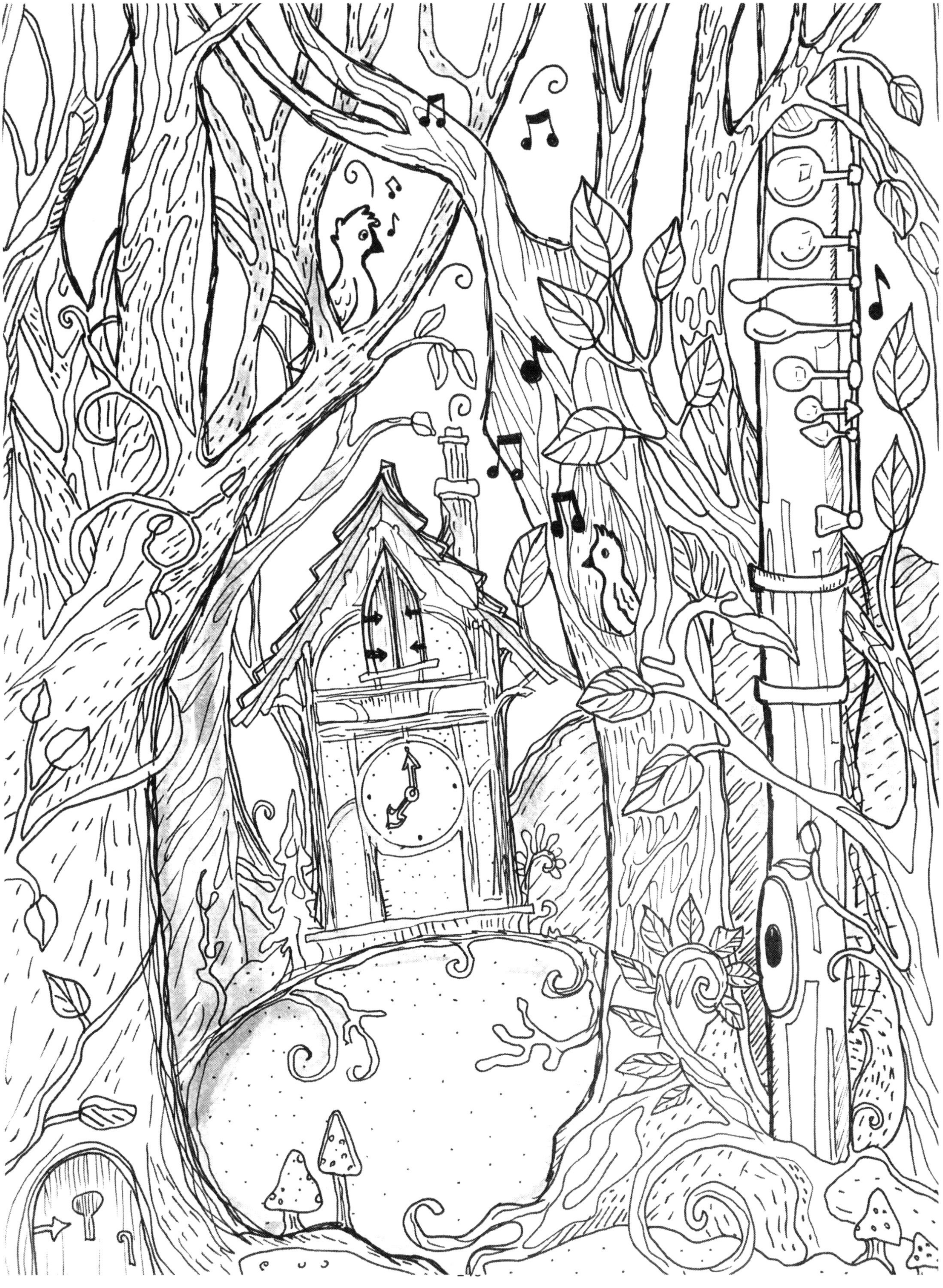

FLY like a
CUCKOO
bird

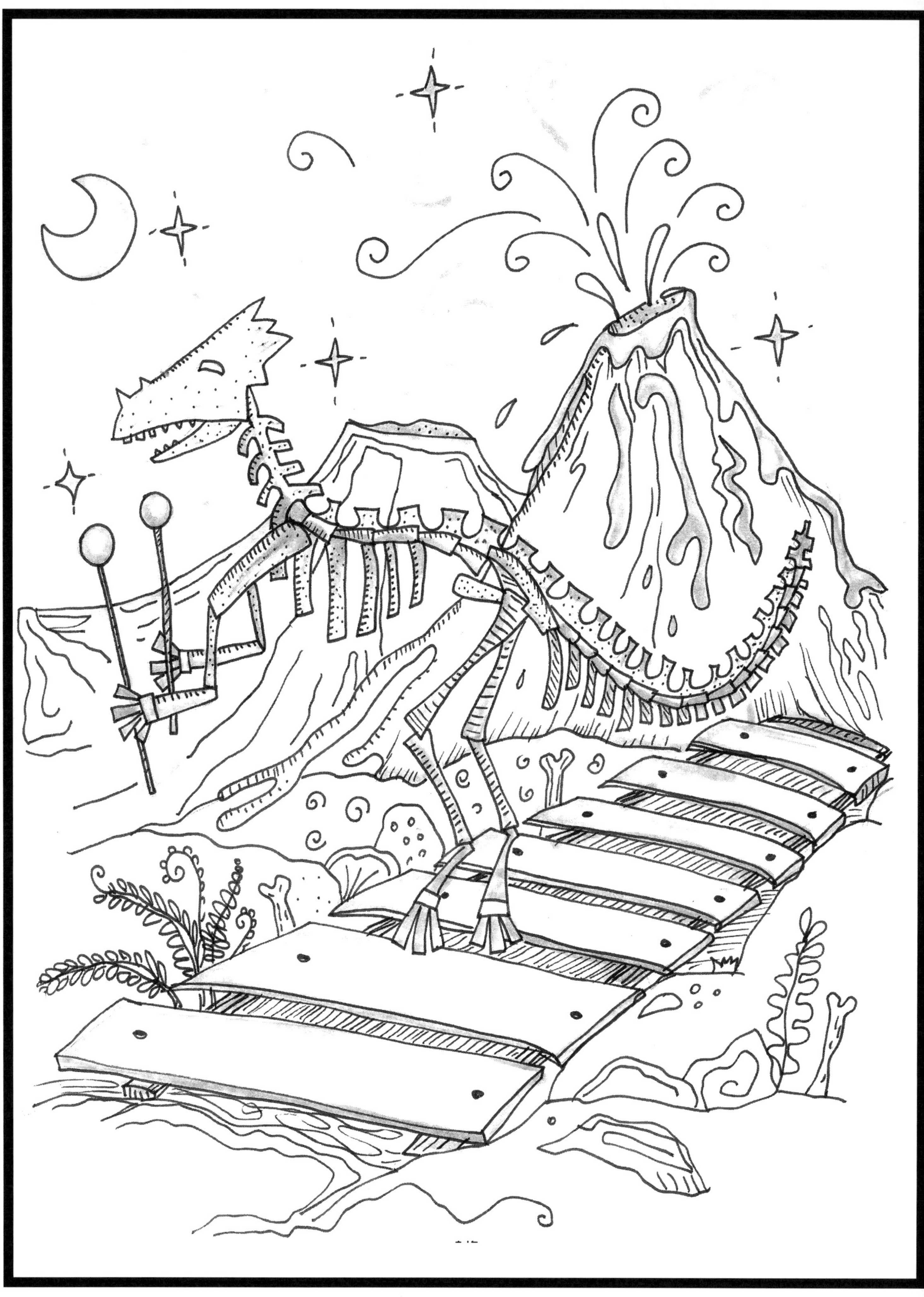

MOVE like the Dinosaur FOSSILS

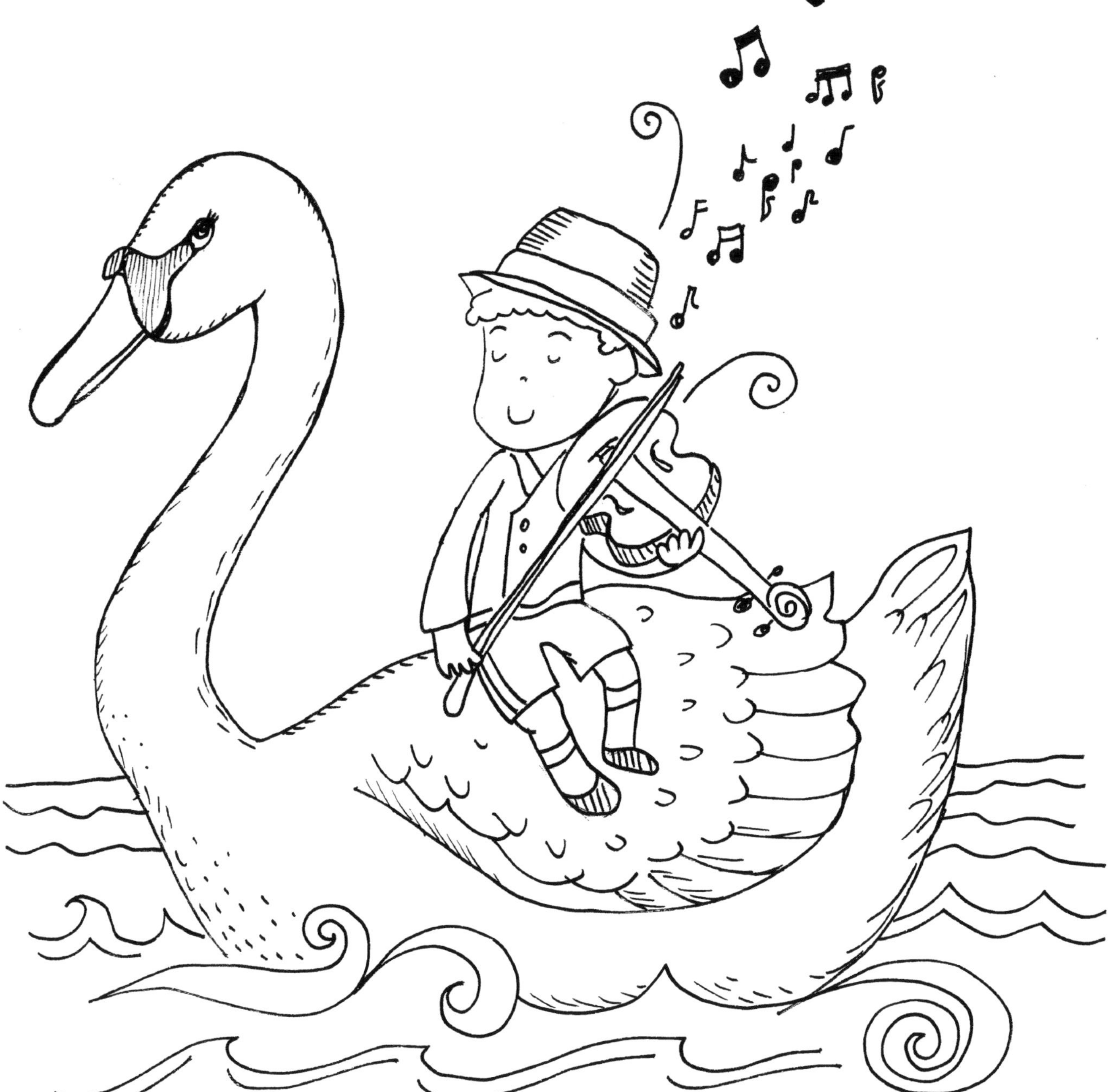

SWIM with THE SWAN

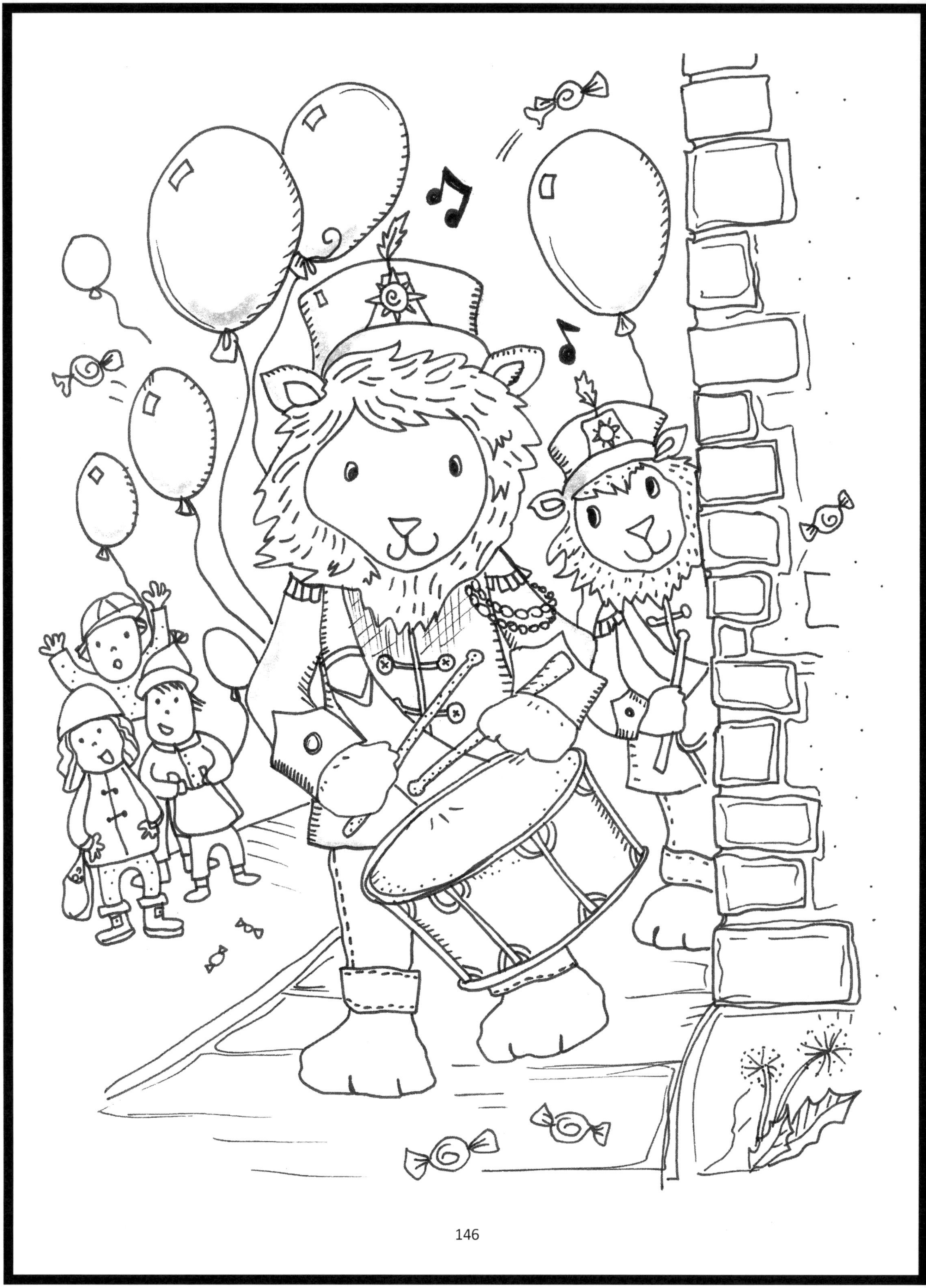

MARCH with the ROYAL LIONS

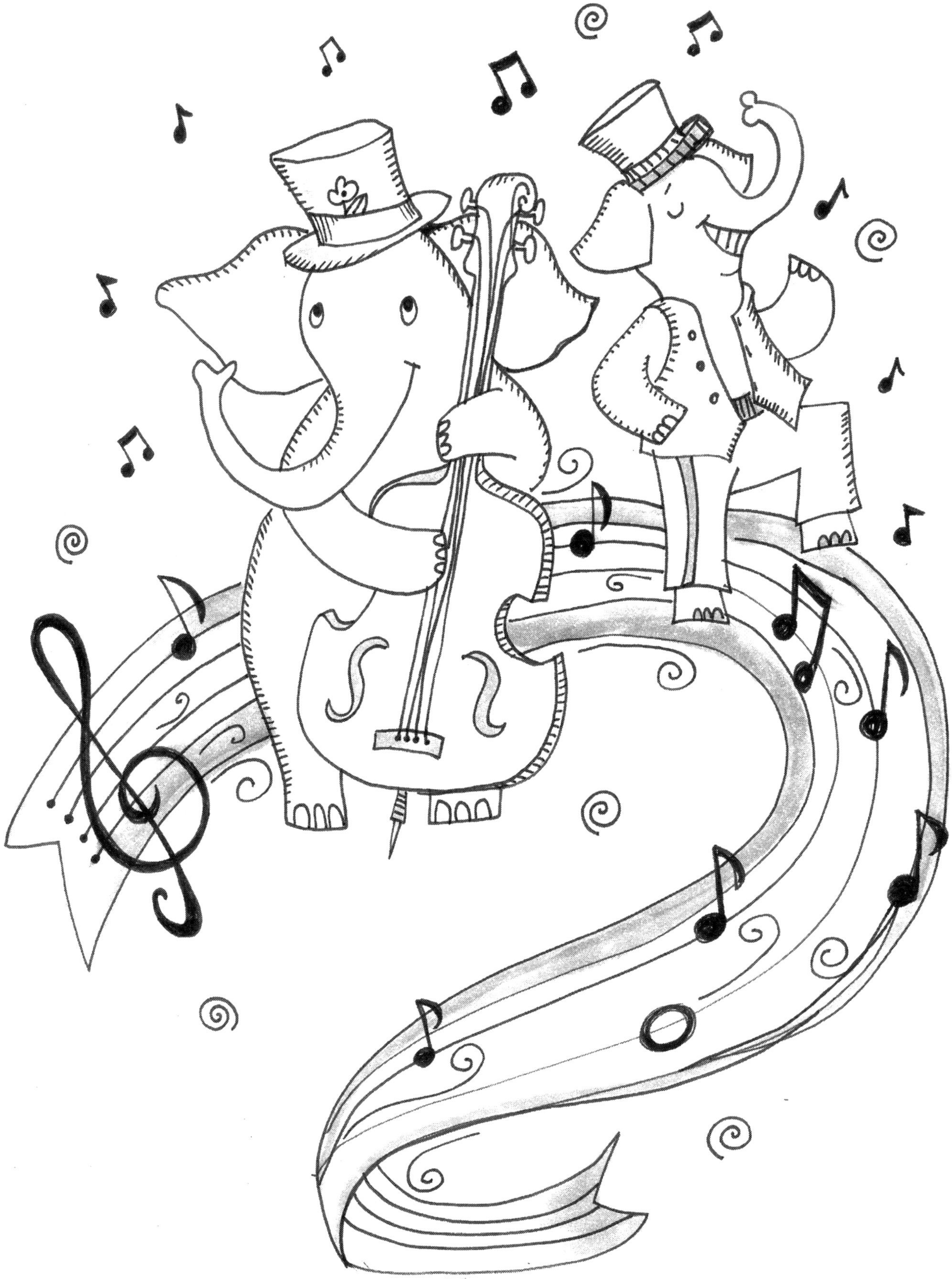

STOMP
like
an ELEPHANT

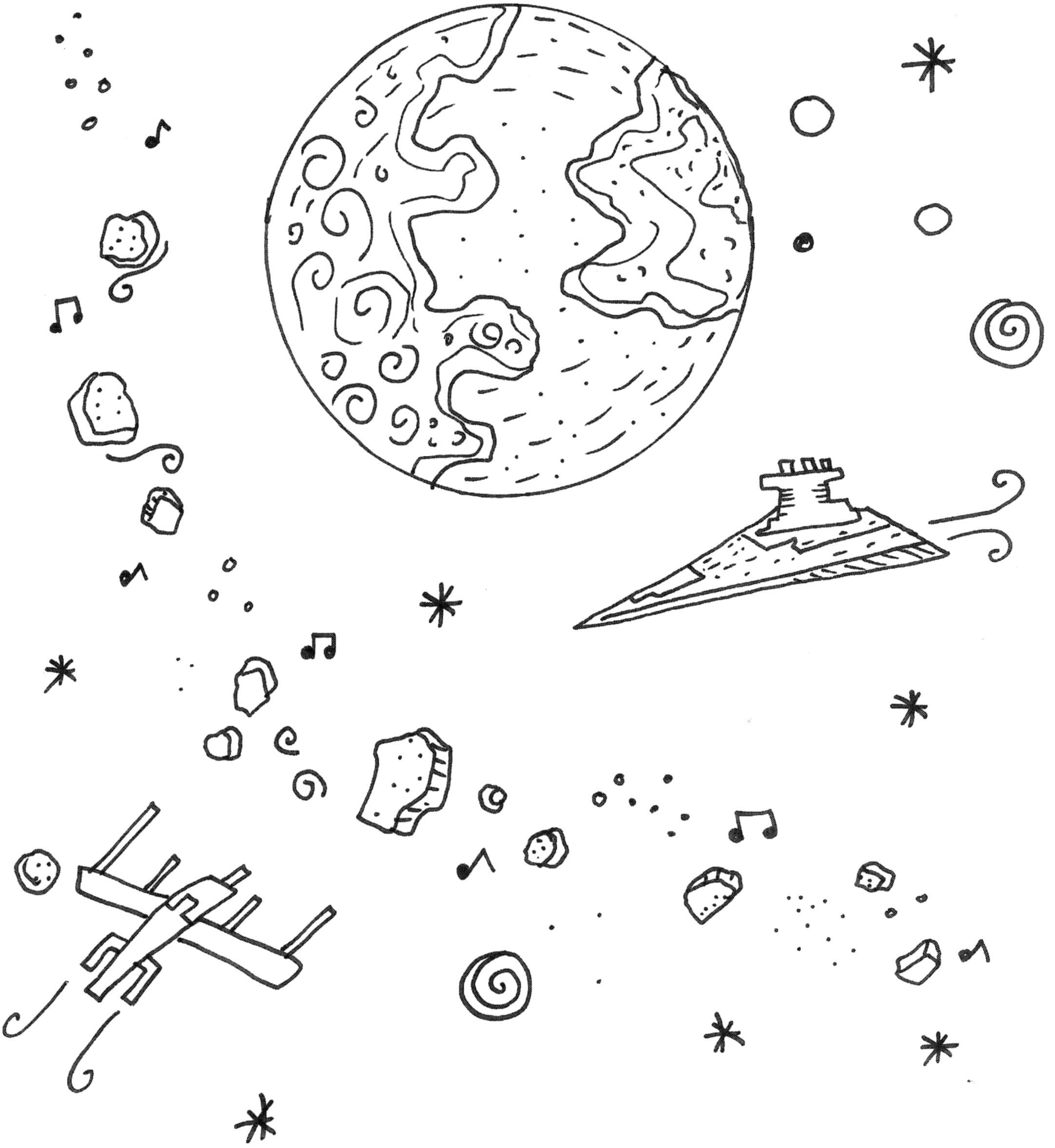

SUPER VILLAIN

Make your own song

LEFT hand C's

"3" finger

RIGHT hand C's and D's

"2's" & "3's"

AWAY IN A MANGER

Away in a manger, no crib for a bed.

The little Lord Jesus laid down his sweet head.

The stars in the sky looked down where he lay.

The little Lord Jesus asleep on the hay.

— James Murray

153

JOY TO THE WORLD

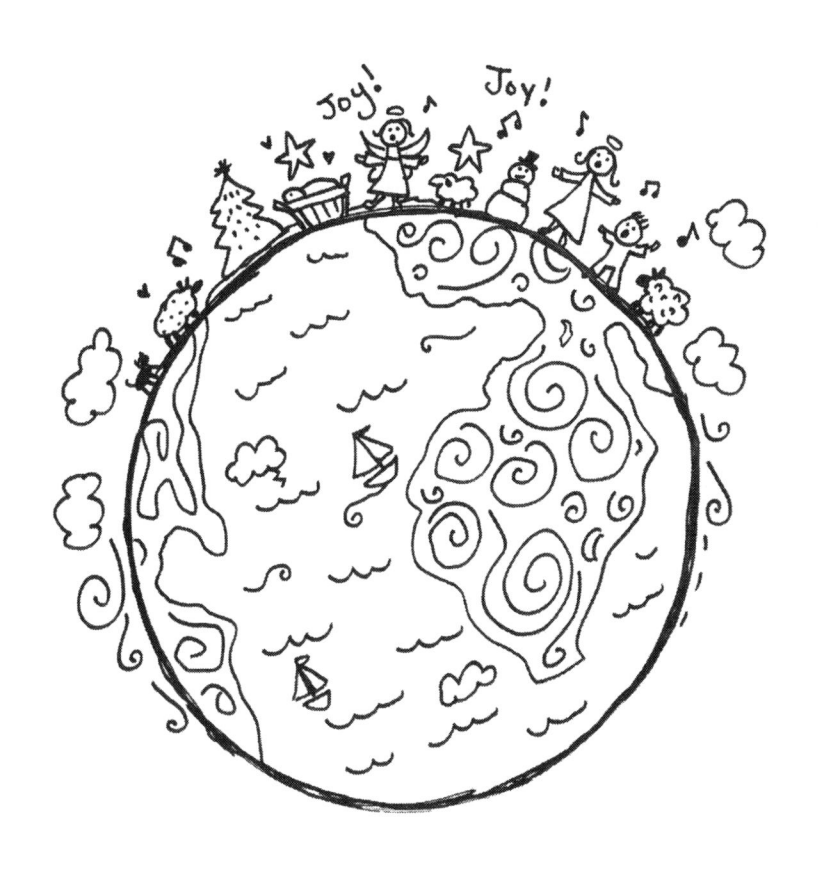

Joy to the world, the Lord is come!

Let earth receive her King;

Let every heart prepare Him room,

And Heaven and nature sing,

And Heaven and nature sing,

And Heaven, and Heaven, and nature sing.

— Isaac Watts

5 4 3 2 2
G F# E D C B A G D
1 2 3 4
3 3 4 4 5 5 5 4 3 2
E E F# F# G G G F# E D
2 1 5 5 4 3 2 2 1
D C B G G F# E D D C B B B B B C
2 2 2 2 2 2 1
2 5 3
D B A A A B C A G G E
2 3 3 3 2 1 3 4
2 1
D C B C B A G
2 1 2 3 4

HAPPY BIRTHDAY TO YOU

Happy birthday to you,

Happy birthday to you,

Happy birthday dear [NAME],

Happy birthday to you!

— Traditional

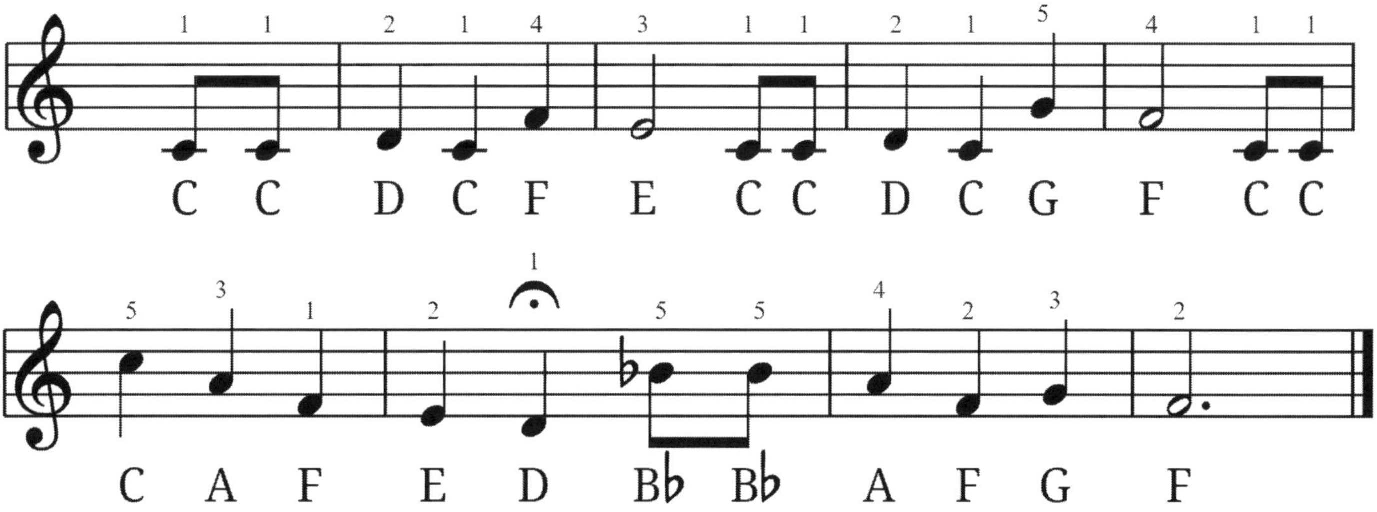
1 1 2 1 4 3 1 1 2 1 5 4 1 1
C C D C F E C C D C G F C C
5 3 1 2 1 5 5 4 2 3 2
C A F E D B♭ B♭ A F G F

MINUET IN G

by J. S. Bach

159

SONGS BY ME

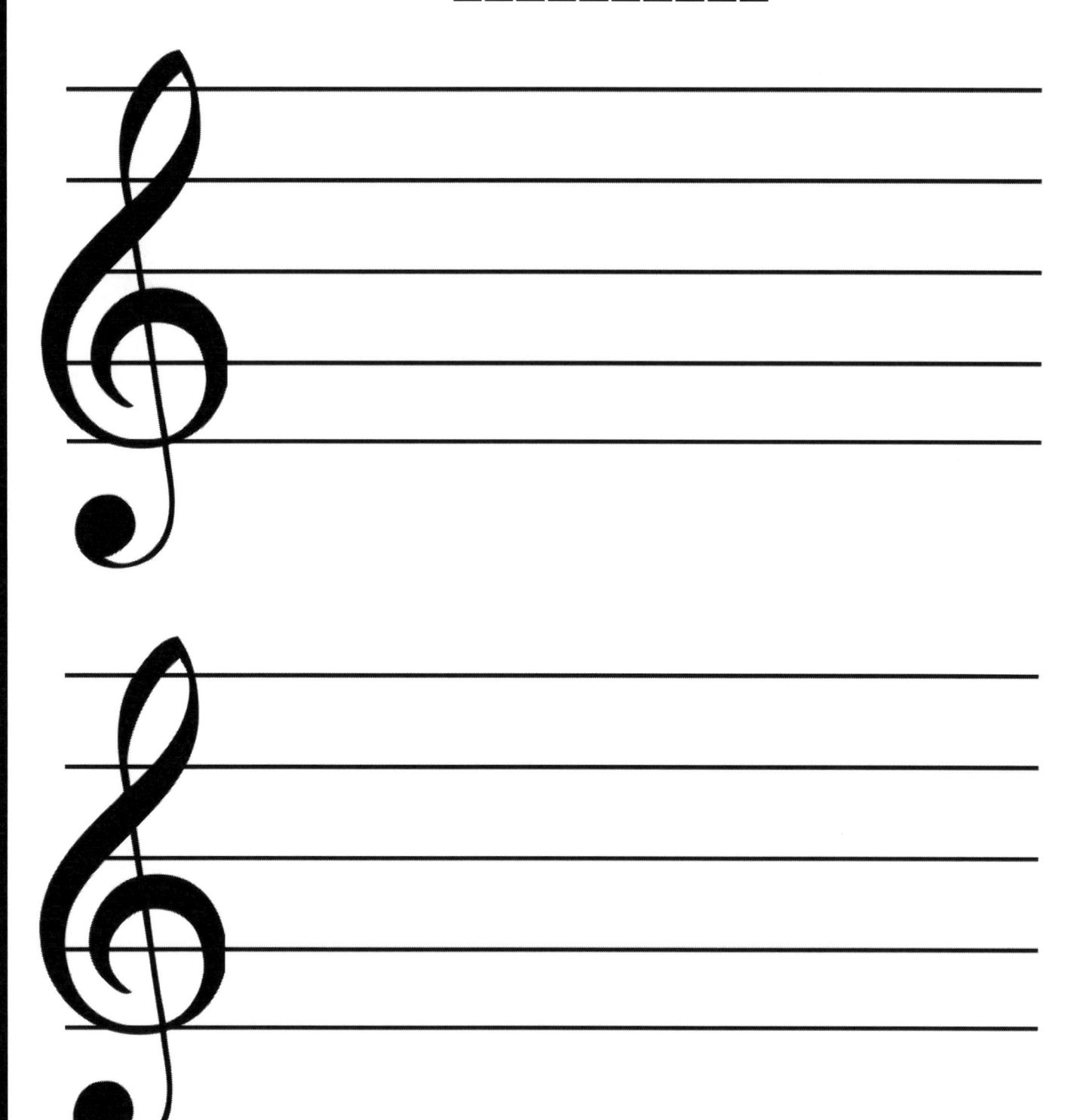

Title:_____

Date:_____

SONGS BY ME

Title:_____

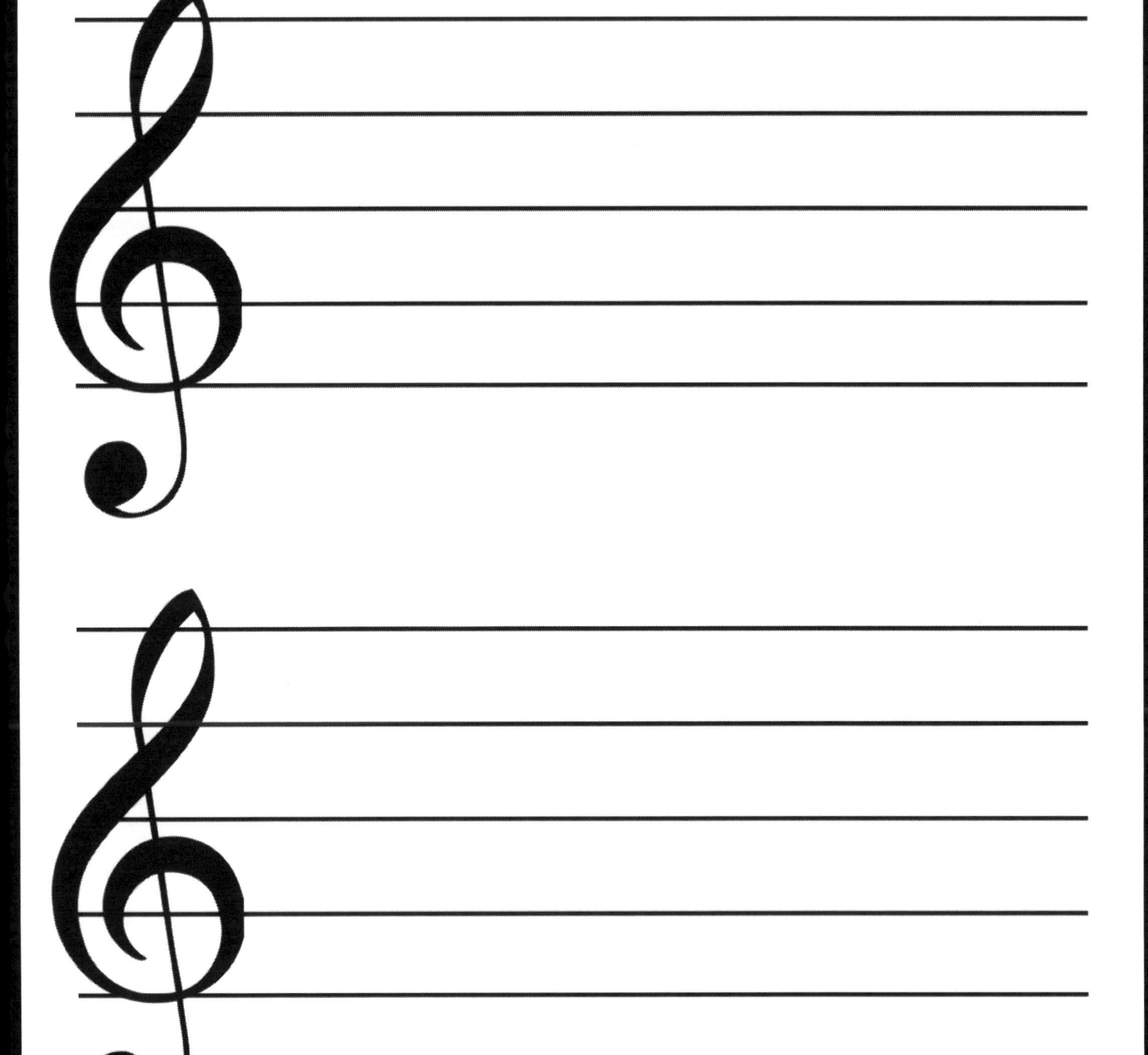

Date:_____

SONGS BY ME

Title:_____

Date:_____

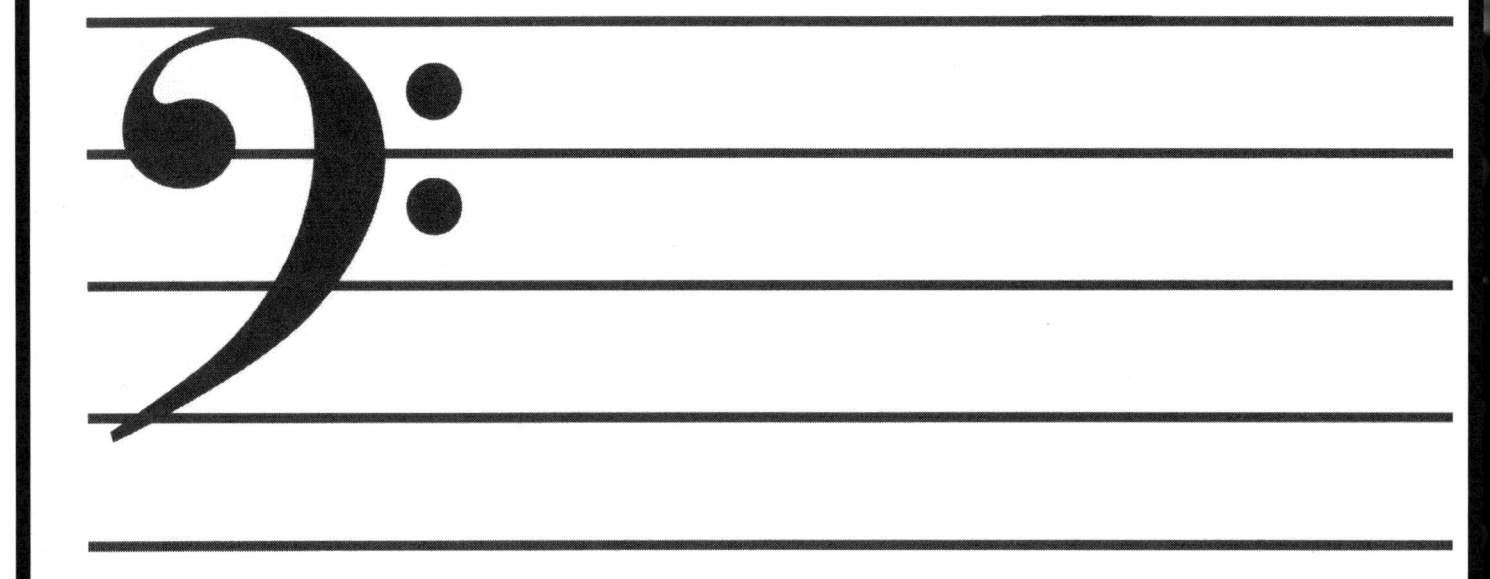

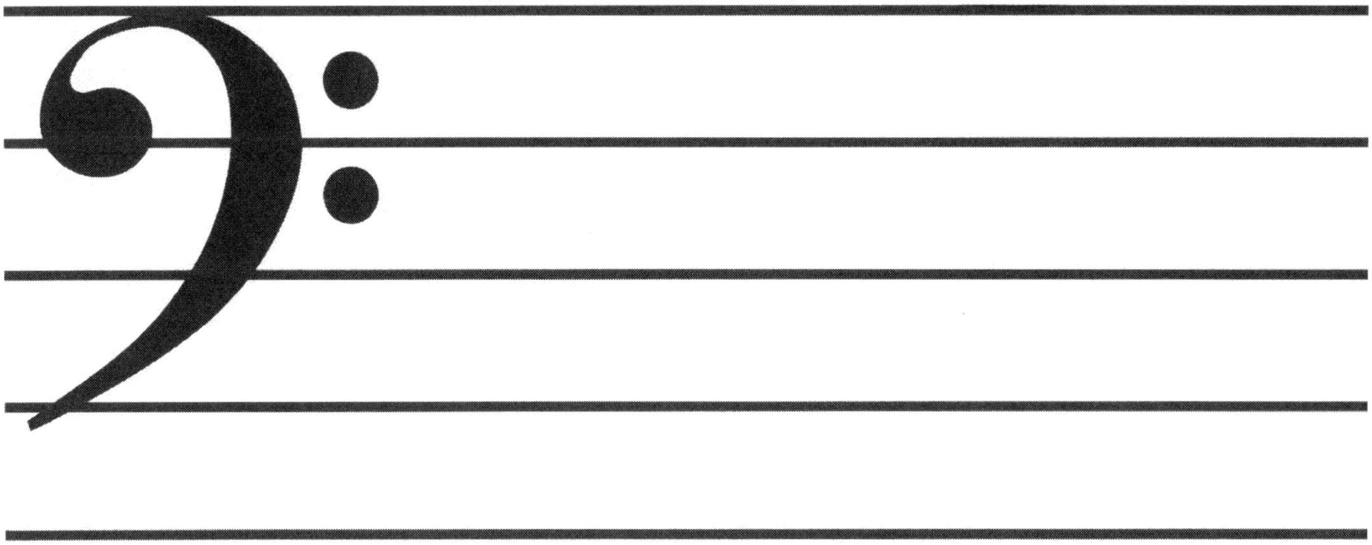

SONGS BY ME

Title:_____

Date:_____

SONGS BY ME

Title:_____

Date:_____

SONGS BY ME

Title:_____

Date:_____

SONGS BY ME

Title:_____

Date:_____

SONGS BY ME

Title:_____

Date:_____

DEDICATION:

This book is dedicated to all my music students, who have kept me young in heart and spirit. I write for children because you have blazed ahead of me on the path of wonder.

And to my family and friends, especially Quinn, Vesper, Brennan, Alistair, and Patrick. Thank you for letting me tag along on your great adventures.

Author: Amber Robinson

Illustrators: Sarah Janisse Brown,

Alexandra Bretush, Anna Kidalova

Aquarium Illustration: Tolik Trishkin

Editing: Aaron J. Robinson

Copyright ©2018 Amber Robinson &

The Thinking Tree, LLC

All Rights Reserved

END NOTES

Herrman, Carlton, Brown & Bass.

I see a Sound: A book of Vocal Exploration.

The Kodály Institute.

Mathias and Sunami.

Sing and Play: Songs and Games for Young Musicians.
Mind Bright and Melody Line Book.

Nimbus Publishers, 1987.

Blank Staves: www.weclipart.com

Keyboard Images: plankchoir.weebly.com/piano-keys.html

Made in the USA
Coppell, TX
12 August 2020